Working With Families of the Mentally Ill

Kayla F. Bernheim, Ph.D.
Anthony F. Lehman, M.D.

W · W · NORTON & COMPANY
New York   *London*

A NORTON PROFESSIONAL BOOK

Published simultaneously in Canada by Penguin Books
Canada Ltd, 2801 John Street, Markham, Ontario L3R 1B4

Printed in the United States of America

Library of Congress Cataloging-in Publication Data

Bernheim, Kayla F.
  Working with families of the mentally ill.

  "A Norton professional book."
  Bibliography: p.
  Includes index.
  1. Mentally ill – Home care. 2. Mentally ill –
Rehabilitation. 3. Mentally ill – Family relationships.
I. Lehman, Anthony F. II. Title.
RC439.5.B48   1985   649'.8   85-18754

ISBN 0-393-70009-7

W. W. Norton & Company, Inc., 500 Fifth Avenue,
New York, N.Y. 10110

W. W. Norton & Company Ltd., 37 Great Russell Street,
London WC1B 3NU

    2 3 4 5 6 7 8 9 0

Dedicated to all of those families who shine with humanity
in the face of an inhumane illness

FOREWORD

A remarkable thing has happened in the past few years in our field – the families of the severely and chronically mentally ill have suddenly banded together on a national level and become an effective mutual support·network as well as a potent political force. After years of stigmatization by themselves, society and, unfortunately, many professionals, they have refused to accept the shame from and blame for their relatives' illnesses and instead sought remedies for the devastating illnesses with which their loved ones are afflicted.

It is ironic that to some extent this incredibly rapid transition has been augmented both by our increasing understanding of the biological underpinnings of psychotic illnesses, emboldening families to refute the "schizophrenogenic" notions of casuality, and by the disastrous movement called "deinstitutionalization" that depopulated our state mental hospitals – throwing many of the mentally ill back into their familial homes or into nearby "community residences" where their appalling condition was more readily visible.

There has recently been any number of publications devoted to schizophrenia and the major affective disorders, traditional forms of family therapy, and family self-help; however, there has been no publication, since the development of this new scientific climate and familial force, to help professionals deal with family members. This book is not about doing *therapy to* families, it is about *working with* them, and as most know, there is a world of difference.

As befits a pioneering work, it tackles the tough issues (such as the theory of expressed emotion, the family's role in causation or maintenance of illness, and confidentiality) forthrightly. By giving professionals the same high quality resource they and others have provided family members, Bernheim and Lehman have filled an important gap in our information bank.

John A. Talbott, M.D.

Professor and Chairman,
Department of Psychiatry,
University of Maryland School of Medicine
Baltimore, MD
September 29, 1985

CONTENTS

II. NUTS AND BOLTS

III. PROFESSIONAL DILEMMAS

APPENDICES

INTRODUCTION

It is nearing the end of a long day at the office, and you are wrapping up your last clinic hour, an intake interview with a young man recently discharged from the state hospital for treatment of chronic schizophrenia. You've reviewed his records, taken a careful history, recorded his mental status, and devised your initial treatment plan. He looks pretty good, has enough medication to last until his next visit, and all in all, you feel that things are well in hand. As you walk him from your office to the reception area, a middle-aged couple approaches you. They introduce themselves as your new patient's parents and tell you that they need desperately to talk with you about his problems since moving home after discharge. They ask about his diagnosis, his medications, question why he was discharged so soon from the hospital, and complain that they have not had a quiet moment for themselves since he returned. Can you please help? You glance at your watch, recalling that you actually expected to get out on time for a change. You wonder how you can possibly respond to all of their questions now and even doubt whether you ought to discuss your patient's condition with them. Where are they coming from? What role do they play in his illness? What should you tell them? What kind of help should you offer?

If this situation and these questions strike a familiar chord for you, then we hope that you will find *Working With Families of the Mentally Ill* helpful. This book is a practical guide to integrating educational, behavioral and supportive techniques to assist families in helping their chronically ill relatives as well as themselves. In it we have attempted to keep our discussions at an applied level, sharing with you things we have found useful as well as problems that have stumped us.

In the first section, Charting a New Course, we begin with a historical discussion of the impact of institutionalization and deinstitutionalization on the families of the mentally ill. Recent studies of the burdens imposed on families by patients who have been discharged from long-term hospitals depict the hardships and stresses families face in the current era of deinstitutionalization. The general failure of our current treatment system to respond to families' needs constitutes an imperative for change in how we work with the chronically mentally ill. The family's plight is described by their emotional turmoil, role confusion, conflict, negative social interactions, and problems in planning. The clinician can help by clarifying the family members' tasks, educating them about the illness and its treatment, and providing support and reassurance. This first section ends with a review of recently devised and successful psychoeducational programs for families of the mentally ill.

Our second section, Nuts and Bolts, addresses the common steps and approaches to helping these families. We describe handling the initial contact with family members, educating them about the illness and treatment, and helping them create a supportive home environment, develop strategies to deal with patients' common behavioral problems, and, last but not least, take care of their own needs. We illustrate all of these steps with extensive clinical examples and end this section with a discussion of how family members can become educated consumers of mental health services and responsible advocates for their ill relatives.

In the final section, Professional Dilemmas, we turn from clinical techniques to professional problems and issues faced by clinicians who choose to work with families of the seriously mentally ill. We generally assume that most families can use information, support, and practical advice to improve their capacities to cope. However, from time to time every clinician has encountered particularly difficult families. We begin this last section with a discussion of some such families, providing some suggestions for working with them and pointing out the risks for the clinician from these families in terms of burnout and pessimism about family work in general. We then move on to a discussion of the conflicting loyalties to patients and families that the clinician can experience. How can one resolve issues of confidentiality while maintaining a cooperative alliance with the family? In addition, how does the family clinician deal with biased views about the family held by other treatment members, particularly those who may view the family as the root of the patient's illness? This section ends with our description of the professional and emotional rewards that we have experienced in working with families and our suggestions for how to implement educational and supportive programs for families within various institutional settings.

Our book is for clinicians of all disciplines who work with families of the chronically mentally ill. In particular, we have kept in mind busy clinicians in settings with a significant proportion of chronically ill clientele, such as public clinics and hospitals, but we expect it will also be of value to general outpatient clinicians, many of whose clients may be siblings, children, parents, or spouses of a chronically ill person. We especially hope this book will be used by professionals in training who carry the promise of a better system of care for the chronically mentally ill and their families.

ACKNOWLEDGMENTS

We are, first of all, indebted to our patients and their families, who have been our best teachers. We are grateful to our editors at Norton, Susan E. Barrows and Donald W. Fusting, for their support, encouragement, and honesty. In addition, we thank Elizabeth Hodgdon, R.N., and Kenneth G. Terkelsen, M.D., for their helpful suggestions on various portions of the manuscript. Rosemarie Oppelt and Lois Bradley patiently typed and retyped several drafts of the book. Finally, we could not have written this without the understanding and encouragement of our families. All shortcomings and biases are, of course, our own.

K.F.B.
A.F.L.

I

CHARTING A NEW COURSE

1

FAMILIES AND DEINSTITUTIONALIZATION

Today we stand at a major turning point in the history of care for the chronically mentally ill. During the past three decades the experiment of deinstitutionalization has failed in its efforts to provide care in the community and reintegrate the chronically mentally ill into the mainstream of life. Yet this failure is but one phase of a much longer cycle that began over 150 years ago with the creation of mental asylums. The dramatic failures of these large mental asylums, which were born with the same levels of hope and enthusiasm that marked the birth of deinstitutionalization, as well as the more recent failures of community-based care, leave us at a difficult juncture. While everyone seems to agree that major changes are needed in the system of care for the mentally ill, it remains unclear what direction our society will choose over the next few decades. Will we opt for an era of reinstitutionalization? Will the system of community-based care be revamped to correct the failures of deinstitutionalization? Will a new, as yet only vaguely conceived, system of care emerge? Or will we languish with the status quo due to indecision and uncertainty?

Whatever the next step may be, families of the mentally ill will undoubtedly play a major role, both because of their current responsibilities as the primary caretakers for many of their ill relatives and because of their growing activism through such organizations as the National Alliance for the

Mentally Ill (NAMI). As we shall see, these families, like their ill relatives, have not been well served by the mental health care system, and the time has come for all of us to learn to work more effectively with them.

The following review of the cycle of institutionalization and deinstitutionalization sets the historical context of these families' plight.* It also helps delineate our current responsibility to more effectively assist these families so that they in turn can provide support for their emotionally disturbed relatives, whether or not these patients actually live at home.

TO THE ASYLUM AND BACK

In colonial America, the family, church and community constituted the triad of stability upon which the social order rested (Rothman, 1971). "Odd" relatives were kept at home or boarded at neighbors and supported through church and public community funds. Following the American Revolution and the changes in our nation's social structure that it fostered, national leaders and medical superintendents grew concerned about the apparent rise of deviancy, particularly criminality and mental illness, in the nation. This concern spurred interest in the roots of mental disorders and stimulated the search for solutions for this growing problem. Although the possibility of biological causes for mental disorders was recognized, public attention focused on causes of deviance in the breakdown of social order and the growing complexities of a post-revolutionary culture. This logically led to the creation of asylums that removed patients to isolated, rural areas away from the deleterious effects of modern society.

The asylums also removed patients from their families, who previously had borne much of the responsibility for their care. Families were specifically discouraged from visiting the asylums. This policy arose from the assumption that parents had somehow failed to instill proper moral values in children

*The authors are indebted to Kenneth G. Terkelsen, M.D., for suggesting this historical perspective.

who became mentally ill and had thus contributed to their deviance. There was also concern that emotional contact with families produced periods of acute excitement in patients. Thus, families were partly blamed for their relatives' illness and excluded from their care (Rothman, 1971).

Considerable enthusiasm and pride accompanied the creation of mental asylums and their moral therapy (Rothman, 1971; Talbott, 1978). However, as the nation emerged from the wrenching experience of the Civil War and faced the new challenges of industrialization, as well as mass migration to urban areas and rapid population growth due to immigration, these rural asylums became overcrowded and fell into a long period of custodial care. The custodial mental institutions endured as the predominant site of care for the chronically mentally ill until deinstitutionalization got underway during the late 1950s. This is not to say that significant ideas about reform had not been set forth earlier. In 1908 Clifford Beers wrote *A Mind That Found Itself*, describing his own experiences as a mental hospital patient. He founded the National Committee for Mental Hygiene, which raised the public's consciousness about the plight of the institutionalized mentally ill. Around the same time, short-term psychopathic hospitals, often affiliated with a university or community hospital, began to spring up (Talbott, 1978).

However, true reform in the care of the institutionalized mentally ill came after World War II. This period of change, which we now look back upon with mixed emotions as the era of deinstitutionalization, arose from a number of factors: a heightened awareness of the prevalence of mental disorders, as seen in recruits for the armed services during both World Wars; enthusiasm about the successes of psychiatrists in treating war-related traumatic neuroses; the strong impetus for social reform following World War II; and the discovery of effective antipsychotic medications in the early 1950s (Greenblatt, 1977). The impact has been stunning. The inpatient population of public mental hospitals dropped from 550,000 in 1955 to under 150,000 in 1981, a decline of over 70 percent (Borus, 1981). However, despite some notably successful model community programs (Bachrach, 1980) and success in refocusing national attention on the plight of the chronically mentally ill (Borus, 1981; Lamb, 1981), the failures of deinstitutionalization have eclipsed its achievements. Critics have pointed out that deinstitutionalization has resulted in premature discharge of patients, premature closure or "phase-down" of public mental hospitals, fragmentation of services, failure to provide adequate housing, failure to provide satisfactory mental health and social services, and, last but not least, further rejection of patients by their families and communities due to inappropriate discharges and lack of support services (Borus, 1981; Lamb, 1981; Scherl and Macht, 1979; Ozarin and Scharfstein, 1978; Rachlin, 1978; Bachrach, 1976). Families, along with patients, have suffered under the move from asylums to the community, just as they may have suffered under the move from community to asylum 150 years earlier.

FAMILY BURDEN

Goldman (1982) estimates that approximately 65 percent of patients discharged from mental hospitals return to their families annually, of whom approximately 25 percent, or 250,000, are chronically mentally ill. He identifies this as a major public health issue in need of response, including family-oriented rehabilitative and treatment services, home visiting, relatives' groups, and community support systems.

Considering the magnitude of the problem, there are surprisingly few studies of the burden that discharged mental patients place on their families. Table 1 summarizes some results from available studies. In an early British study, the families of patients referred for psychiatric treatment in two service districts were interviewed regarding the impact of their relative's illness on the family (Grad and Sainsbury, 1968). Approximately two-thirds of the families reported some hardship because of the patient at the time of referral, and one-fifth described the hardship as severe. Severe family burdens were most significantly related to patient's aggression, delusions, hallucinations, confusion, and inability to care for self. Over half of the families attributed mental health problems in other family members to concerns about the patient's illness; most typically these problems manifested themselves as worrying, although more serious symptoms, such as insomnia, headaches, excessive irritability and depression, were also reported. A third of the families experienced restrictions on their leisure and social activities, and 29 percent had their domestic routines upset. A quarter of the families suffered a reduction in family income by at least 10 percent, and in 10 percent of families the reduction in income was over 50 percent. Children were reported to be adversely affected in a third of the families. Throughout a two-year follow-up period approximately one-third of the families still reported hardships attributable to their relative's mental illness in the areas of household routine, social and leisure life, income, and adverse effects on children.

In a subsequent British survey, the patients' behaviors most burdensome to families of chronic schizophrenic patients were social withdrawal, psychotic behaviors, and unpredictability of behaviors (Creer and Wing, 1974). Nearly half felt the problems posed by the patient's illness had been detrimental to the health or well-being of other family members.

Surveys of families of the mentally ill in the United States have yielded results similar to those of the British studies. Doll (1976) interviewed relatives of 125 patients recently discharged from state hospitals. Using a sentence completion questionnaire, he evaluated family members' attitudes about having their mentally ill relative at home. He found that the families often displayed a high level of tolerance for deviant behaviors, but the burden experienced by families was substantial and clearly related to the severity of the patient's symptoms. Two-thirds of the relatives of patients with serious symptoms felt shame, compared to only 35 percent of the relatives of less disturbed patients. Of those families of less severely disturbed relatives, only 27 percent reported that the patient's illness posed financial burdens or disrupted the

TABLE 1
Impact of Patients on Family Burden

Study	Method	Levels of Family Burden
Grad & Sainsbury, 1968	Comparison of family burden for 410 patients referred for psychiatric services in two service areas, one (Chichester) with more extensive community services than the other (Salisbury). Follow-up after two years.	*Chichester Salisbury* *At Referral* None 40% 29% Some 42% 46% Severe 18% 25% *At Two Year Follow-Up* None 64% 81% Some 27% 13% Severe 9% 6%
Creer and Wing, 1974	Interviews with 80 relatives of schizophrenic patients, 80% with major behavioral disturbances.	Minimal – 20% Severe – 50%
Doll, 1976	Survey of 125 families of patients recently discharged from state hospitals, comparing those with high vs. low symptom disturbances.	*Symptom Levels* *High Low* Shame 67% 35% Financial Burden 72% 27% Feeling Trapped 67% 41%
Hatfield, 1978	Survey of 89 relatives of schizophrenic patients.	Effects of patient's illness on family: Hardship for siblings 27% Threat to parents' marriage 20% Disrupts family's social life 17%

8

Endicott et al., 1978 Herz et al., 1979	Comparison of brief (11 days) vs. standard (60 days) hospitalization. One-year and two-year follow-ups.	Disrupts personal life of family members		14%
		Stress		65%
		Anxiety		30%
		Resentment		24%
		Grief and depression		22%
		No significant group differences at follow-up.		
			% of Respondents@	
		Burden	1 year	2 years
		Worry	73%	55%
		Careful not to upset patient	52%	47%
		Less income	42%	40%
		Patient argues	24%	10%
		Patient uncooperative	25%	25%
Test & Stein, 1980	Comparison of innovative community treatment program (TCL) with standard hospitalization and aftercare. Follow-up at four months.	Burden	TCL	Standard
		Work Missed	22%	20%
		Disruption of social/leisure time	14%	11%
		Disruption of domestic routine	5%	17%
Reynolds & Hoult, 1984	Same as Test & Stein, 1980. One-year follow-up.	Follow-up Burden	TCL	Standard
		Support and information from treatment system adequate	88%	39%
		Coping better	69%	28%
		No worry	48%	38%

family's daily routine, compared to 72 percent of the families with severely disturbed patients. Although 83 percent of all relatives said that they wanted the patient to come home, this was true in only 42 percent of families with a seriously symptomatic relative. Over 70 percent of the families who desired to exclude patients from their social lives had severely disturbed relatives. Finally, two-thirds of families with highly symptomatic relatives felt trapped by the patient's presence, compared to 41 percent of less disturbed patients' families. Doll concluded that patients do place significant burden on their families and generate strong feelings of bitterness and pain, even though the families are often willing to tolerate the patient's presence at home.

Hatfield discovered similar patterns of family burden in her survey of family members in the Schizophrenia Association of Greater Washington (Hatfield, 1978). The majority of families were experiencing disruptions at home due to patients' bizarre and abnormal behaviors, intrusive and disturbing behaviors, or poor task functioning, such as poor personal care and lack of motivation. Stress constituted the most common emotional response in the family (65 percent), followed by anxiety (30 percent), resentment (24 percent), and grief and depression (22 percent). The patients' illness caused hardship for siblings in 27 percent, posed a threat to the parents' marriage in 20 percent, and disrupted the family's social life in 17 percent. She concluded that families of schizophrenics at home struggle under formidable emotional burdens and need social supports and services to reduce their distress.

In a study of brief versus standard length hospitalization for psychiatric patients (averages of 11 days and 60 days, respectively), Endicott and colleagues found no significant differences in family burden between the two groups (Endicott, Herz, and Gibbon, 1978; Herz, Endicott, and Gibbon, 1979). At the end of one year after hospitalization, families continued to experience significant family burden related to the patient's illness. Over 70 percent were worried about the future, and 52 percent said they had to be careful not to upset the patient. In 42 percent of families, patients continued to contribute less money to the family than if well, and in nearly a third other family members had to assume some of the patient's previous responsibilities. These patterns persisted through two years of follow-up. On only a few family burden items were differences found in relation to length of hospital stay, and these usually favored the brief stay treatment. The investigators concluded that length of hospitalization within the range studied had little effect on family burden. These findings related to family burden, combined with other findings showing no major outcome advantages to standard length hospitalizations compared to brief hospitalization, supported the investigators' conclusion that hospital stays can be shortened without significant negative impact on patient outcome or family burden. However, the data also support previous studies showing that patients frequently impose major burdens on their families when out of the hospital.

Test and Stein (1980; Stein and Test, 1980) assessed the social cost to families of two alternative treatment programs for chronically disabled psychiatric patients. In their study patients who sought admission to a state hospital were randomly assigned to either standard treatment, which consisted of short-term hospitalization (median of 17 days) and outpatient aftercare, or their experimental Training in Community Living (TCL) program, which provided intensive community-based treatment. The TCL program encompassed around-the-clock outpatient services and aggressive outreach to patients and families in their community environments. One-year patient outcomes, measured by time spent in hospital, employment rates, life satisfaction, and psychiatric symptoms, all favored the TCL program. However, no significant differences in family burden were found between the two groups. The alternative community-based program, like shortened hospital stays (Endicott et al., 1979), did not seem to increase the families' burden, but it also failed to decrease it, despite a very impressive and innovative approach to treatment.

A replication of Stein and Test's Training in Community Living Program has occurred in Australia (Reynolds and Hoult, 1984). Patients presenting for hospital admission were randomly assigned to either standard psychiatric hospital care with outpatient aftercare or the TCL program. Standard hospital care lasted on average three weeks. The TCL program again consisted of intensive, 24-hour community-based care with active outreach of the treatment team to the families' homes as needed. At 12-month follow-up the results revealed a marked reduction in hospital-based care among the TCL patients compared to controls. Families were clearly more satisfied with the TCL program than with the standard treatment. Compared to the relatives of standard treatment patients, those of TCL patients were more likely to feel that they had received enough support and information (39 percent vs. 88 percent), and that they were coping better (28 percent vs. 69 percent). There was a statistically nonsignificant trend for TCL families to experience less burden due to the patient's illness after one year. However, as with the Stein and Test program, there were no significant differences between the two treatment groups on any measures of objective burdens, such as disruption to work, social life, or daily routines.

In summary, the burdens imposed by mental patients on their families in the era of deinstitutionalization are considerable. Innovative community-based programs that maintain patients out of the hospital and improve patient outcome seem to produce about the same amount of family burden as standard hospital treatment plus aftercare. Since the lengths of stay for the standard treatments in the available studies are still short, usually less than two months, compared to lengths of stay in the days of custodial institutional care, it is not possible to estimate how much family burden could be alleviated by longer hospitalizations. However, longer hospitalizations exact their own tolls on patients, as well documented in earlier critiques of custodial care (Goffman, 1961; Wing, 1962) and are extremely expensive. We can say with some confidence that, within the range of currently acceptable lengths of hospital stay, family burden does not seem to be affected significantly by how much time the patient spends in the hospital. If family burdens are to be reduced, something more is needed.

FAMILIES' NEEDS AND
PROFESSIONAL RESPONSES

Evidence exists that professionals have not adequately addressed the needs of families of the mentally ill. Hatfield (1978) reports that nearly half of the families she contacted complained that mental health services had no value for them. In a subsequent survey (Hatfield, 1979), she reported that families prioritized their needs as follows (see Table 2): a better understanding of the patient's symptoms, suggestions about how to cope with problem behaviors, opportunities to relate to other families with similar problems, family respite from the patient at times, a place other than home in which the patient can live, more understanding from relatives and friends, financial relief, and therapy for themselves. In her most recent study (Hatfield, 1983), she found that the areas in which therapists were perceived least favorably by families were keeping the family appraised about what is going on (35 percent rated as poor) and lack of sympathy for family suffering (28 percent rated as poor). She found no significant

TABLE 2
What Families Want*

Better understanding of symptoms – 57%
Specific suggestions for coping with patient's
    behavior – 55%
Relating to people with similar experiences – 44%
Substitute care, for family respite – 30%
Having patient change place of living – 27%
More understanding from relatives and friends – 18%
Relief from financial distress – 18%
Therapy for self – 12%

Usual sources of support and help
    Friends – 84%
    Family – 73%
    Therapy – 55%

*From Hatfield, 1979

relationship between the families' priorities for help and the focus of their family therapy.

Holden and Lewine (1982) found similar levels of family dissatisfaction with mental health services (see Table 3). In their survey of families in five different locales in the United States, families reported that professionals increased their feelings of guilt, confusion, and frustration. One-third felt that their contacts with the professional were not helpful. Over half stated that the professional had not involved them in therapy. Two-thirds felt that their contacts with the professional were too infrequent and expressed a lack of confidence in the patient's therapist. Half had not received information about the patient's need for medication and two-thirds were dissatisfied with the patient's medications. The net result was that 74 percent were dissatisfied with the services received. Major sources of dissatisfaction included lack of information about the diagnosis and treatment, vague and evasive professional responses, professional avoidance of labeling the illness (which increased their confusion), lack of support during the period of the patient's transition back to the community, lack of help in finding community resources, and little or no advice about how to cope with the patient's symptoms and problem behaviors. Here are some of the families' comments.

TABLE 3
How Families Feel About Professional Services*

Family member's primary response to mental health
    professional:
        Frustration – 38%
        Not helpful – 33%
        Very or generally satisfied with service – 26%
        Powerlessness – 13%
        Learning of coping strategies – 9%
        Confidence – 8%

---

*From Holden and Lewine, 1982

[For professionals] to proceed on the assumption that the illness is caused by malparenting is very damaging because these attitudes are transmitted by innuendo if not directly. This results in increased guilt felt by the parents and decreased ability to accept the diagnosis and impairment. (Holden and Lewine, 1982, p. 627)

Each doctor seemed to make a different decision, and I was never helped to understand why. I'm not sure what to think. I was left in the dark. Everything was frightening because unexplained. (p. 628)

I would like consultations about what I could realistically expect of my son. (p. 629)

There is no help available until after an aggressive act has occurred. (p. 630)

The person (patient's therapist) was only one among many professionals in connection with my daughter's illness. A few of them were very good; many were atrociously badly trained and insensitive. (Hatfield, 1983, p. 54)

Although there is considerable consistency across these surveys, they are methodologically limited when it comes to generalizing the findings, since all were surveys of members of family self-help organizations. Typically, respondents were well-educated, white mothers of schizophrenics. One might expect members of such groups to be more dissatisfied with available professional services than other families, although to our knowledge no data exist in regard to this issue. Despite this limitation, these survey results at the very least constitute a strong stimulus for us to reexamine how we view and treat these families.

WHAT CAN BE DONE?

The clinician interested in helping families of the chronically mentally ill faces a difficult task. Clearly neither institutionalization nor deinstitutionalization has achieved optimal results for patients or their families. It seems unlikely that any dramatic changes will occur in the near future either in the system of care for these patients or in our ability to cure serious mental disorders, despite impressive progress in understanding some of the biological bases of such illnesses as schizophrenia and affective disorders (Henn and Nasrallah, 1982; Paykel, 1982). Theories about the families' role in the etiology of major psychiatric disorders have fallen under serious criticism (Goldstein and Rodnick, 1975; Terkelsen and Cole, 1984), and some family therapists have expressed concern that traditional approaches to family treatment based upon these etiologic theories at times have done more harm than good (Terkelsen, 1983; Grunebaum, 1984).

Still, when faced with a seriously mentally ill patient and a concerned, upset, confused, overburdened—and yet caring—family, we feel compelled to help somehow. At the very least, we can provide information, emotional support, and acknowledgment that family members have their own needs. This approach, termed supportive family counseling (Bernheim, 1982), is analogous to the support one may offer to the family of a patient with a serious and chronic medical illness (Ahlfield, Soler, and Marcus, 1983; Haley, 1983; Brody, 1985; Pinkston and Linsk, 1984; Clark and Rakowski, 1983; Cantor, 1983; Worden, 1982; Wilshaw and Alpin, 1981; Adams-Greenly and Moynihan, 1983). Such illnesses can exact severe emotional and financial tolls on families, taxing the family members' ability to cope and demanding a redefinition of their roles and expectations. Medical care may focus on alleviating certain symptoms but often neglects the needs of the family members and the role they will be asked to play in the care of the chronically ill patient, even if the patient does not return home. For us, whether the patient has diabetes, heart disease, epilepsy, stroke, cancer, or a chronic mental illness makes little difference when it comes to being responsive to the family. Supportive family counseling offers a generic approach which, as you will see, draws upon educational, behavioral, and supportive techniques. It recognizes that the patient's illness has profound effects on the family, and that the family's responses to the patient can have a major impact on the patient's subsequent adjustment. Supportive family counseling seeks to help both the family and the patient by means of information, support, understanding, and concrete advice about how to help each other.

2

THE FAMILY'S PLIGHT

The presence of a chronically mentally ill family member has a profoundly disruptive, disorganizing effect on family life. The family is faced with the challenge of providing for the needs of its ill member while negotiating the inevitable conflicts among its healthy members, all within an atmosphere fraught with confusion, stigma, and secrecy. In this chapter, we begin by describing the common effects of chronic mental illness on the family. We then move to a discussion of the tasks family members face in providing for their ill member and for themselves, and finish by outlining the needs of families with respect to professional intervention.

EMOTIONAL EFFECTS

The emotional anguish suffered by parents, siblings, children, and spouses of the mentally ill can hardly be overstated. For parents (and, to a lesser extent, other family members), guilt represents a common and substantial hurdle to overcome before effective coping can take place. The past several decades have witnessed an emphasis on environmental determinism both in the psychological and psychiatric literature and in the public press. In short, it is common (although faulty) knowledge that crazy children are invariably produced by crazy, bad, or, at the very least, incompetent parents. Accompanying the guilt that parents inevitably feel is a wish to compensate the ill child for the presumed wrongs of the past; while entirely understandable, this can have a negative impact on the parents' ability to effectively set limits or develop realistic expectations.

Husbands or wives who are aware that their spouse's illness predated the marriage may be less susceptible to the feeling that they caused the illness than parents of a mentally ill child or spouses of those whose first symptoms appeared following marriage. However, they may still berate themselves for mismanaging their spouse, for being unsupportive or short-tempered, or for being the cause of a particular episode of renewed symptoms. They may also feel guilty about bringing children into a difficult situation when they "should have known better."

Children whose parents suffer from chronic mental illness and siblings of ill family members may also be guilt-ridden. Typically, they are concerned about having had angry, hateful thoughts about the ill member or about having caused the illness by some other shortcoming in themselves.

Family members search for an explanation of the illness outside of their own behavior as well, and are often plagued with feelings of anger – at the ill relative who is often seen as malingering or manipulative, at other family members, at the ineffective professional "helpers," at unsupportive extended family or friends, at God. Typically, anger and guilt go hand in hand, as one leads to the other in a painful, debilitating cycle.

Equally painful is the sense of loss, of grieving, that accompanies the growing awareness that the ill relative may never meet his own or others' expectations. One mother put it this way:

> It was really like a period of mourning, and I realized that it was. It was giving up the goals and the picture of her as a normal adult functioning, working at a library, which had been her dream. I think that's what it was – giving up that picture of her as an adult. (Bernheim, Lewine, and Beale, 1982, p. 31)

Of course, with a chronically mentally ill relative the mourning process is never completed; rather, periods of relative

quiet and acceptance are interspersed with episodes of renewed grief, stimulated, perhaps, by the accomplishment of
a peer, or a birthday, or some other seemingly innocuous
event.

> Living continually with a chronically ill individual en-
> sures that you maintain a little bit of hope, no mat-
> ter how ill the person. It is difficult to obtain a final
> peacefulness. . . . You sit in the car together, you go
> places and do things together, but all the while it is
> not the relative you once knew. The conflict between
> physical life and dead hopes is constantly there.
> (Bernheim et al., 1982, p. 32)

Finally, anxiety may be a consuming, ever-present sensa-
tion. Typically, families relate the experience of waking up
each morning with feelings ranging from discomfort to dread.
Will the ill person yell at hallucinated voices in the super-
market today? Will a sibling get angry or frustrated and
storm out of the house? Will a spouse and the patient get into
a fight about medication? What will I say if my neighbor
asks, "How is everything going?" While evening may bring
some relief, sleep is often disrupted by anticipatory anxiety
about tomorrow.

Fears that the patient may hurt himself or someone else
are common:

> There are no mental vacations. Even when you are
> physically away from the ill person, you are thinking
> about her, "Is she all right? Should I call to check?
> Did she remember to shut off the stove after cook-
> ing dinner? Did she wander out in the middle of the
> night?" (Bernheim et al., 1982, p. 76)

Since the affective disorders, schizophrenia, and several of
the personality disorders do have elevated suicide rates, and
since impaired judgment and poor self-care skills are common, such fears are not without basis in fact.

There are also fears for the future. Will the family member ever improve? What will happen when caretakers grow old and die? When will the next relapse come? How severe will it be? Will the family be able to manage it successfully? Will yet another involuntary admission finally alienate the patient from the family?

Siblings and children have a special fear: "Will it happen to me?" While often unvoiced, these fears can have powerful effects on the development of self-image and self-esteem and on the willingness to take risks and to commit oneself to a course of action. These family members also worry about the possibility that the burden of caretaking will shift to them in the future. "If my father dies, how will I manage the care of my ill mother and my own life as well?" Such concerns can lead to increasingly distancing oneself (both physically and emotionally) from the family or to putting off investment in personal goals indefinitely as one waits for the axe to fall.

Thus, having a mentally ill relative provokes powerful feelings in family members, no two of whom have exactly the same concerns or share the same point of view. However, the effects of chronic mental illness on family life are far more extensive.

ROLE CONFUSION

Role confusion, the inability to count on all family members to do their own chores and live up to expectations, is a common feature of these families (Beale, 1982). If, for example, the husband/father in a family has a chronic mental illness, the wife may find that he is unable to provide the financial and emotional support usually provided by a husband. Their sexual relationship and sense of intimacy are likely to be impaired. Further, she may have to take on some of his parenting functions, in addition to her own. She may discover that her responsibilities are those of a single parent, but without the freedom of decision-making that single parenting provides. She may also have to take on quasi-parental functions with respect to her husband, such as monitoring his symptoms, his medications, and his hospitalizations. This kind of situation may be further complicated by the fluctuating course of the illness. For example, the husband's sexual interest may wax and wane, as may his capacity for work, participation in household routines, and emotional availability. Thus, the wife is at risk for ongoing confusion and resentment, since the demands for flexibility are much greater than would normally be expected.

The children in such a family discover that Dad cannot be expected to engage in normal fathering activities. They may also have to take on certain caretaking functions, like keeping an eye on Dad when Mom is at work. They may find that mother looks to them for emotional support and possibly even for advice. In short, they may be called upon to fulfill adult roles when they are ill-equipped to do so and may be confused as to where the power resides in the family. They are certain to have reduced time and energy to engage in the normal developmental tasks of childhood and adolescence.

When an adult child has a chronic mental illness, parents may be unable to give up the parenting role at the usual time. Further, they may ask their other adult children to take on some of this function, particularly with reference to future caretaking when they themselves die or become incapacitated. In this situation, brothers and sisters often feel great resentment toward their sibling who has sapped their parents' energies, failed to be the older (or younger) brother or sister they had wished for, embarrassed them in their adolescence by disordered behavior, and will be a burden to them in their adulthood when they also have to care for their own nuclear families. Regardless of which family member is ill, role relationships must undergo some compensatory shift.

MAGNIFICATION OF CONFLICT

The presence of a mentally ill member tends to both provoke conflict between other family members and magnify the normal conflicts that might occur in any case. For example, most spouses have differing styles of parenting with respect to provision of structure, displays of affection, level of expectations, and tolerance for mistakes. In families in which children grow up with good adaptive skills, these differences are minimized by the parents. There is no tremendous investment in being "right" or "wrong" because no serious problems have arisen. When a child is mentally ill, however, these normal differences in style tend to become loaded with surplus importance, as the parents search for the cause of the disorder in their own and each other's behavior and struggle desperately to "do the right thing" as situations arise.

Conflicts between the well siblings and the parents are almost unavoidable. Commonly, parental attempts to shelter the well children from the emotional fallout in the family are read by the children as robbing them of their due. For example, one family suggested that their daughter might want to visit a friend during college vacation rather than come home, since her mentally ill brother (with whom she was in significant conflict and whose symptoms were under poor control) would be home. The parents felt that they were sacrificing for her, but she felt that she was being sacrificed for her brother.

Well siblings are often enraged over their parents' "taking it" from the ill sibling. Unconstrained by the kinds of emotional ties the parents feel, and somewhat out of touch with the reality issues involved in securing treatment and/or hospitalization for a resistant person, well siblings are often angry that their parents do not find some way to protect the family once and for all from the chaos that the illness generates. Parents, in return, may feel disappointed and hurt that the well siblings do not show more understanding for their sick brother or sister or at least for their parents' plight.

SOCIAL EFFECTS

While each family member privately suffers from a host of painful feelings, and while conflict in the family provokes disorganization and lack of cohesion, social effects of the illness are taking place as well. Typically, families find that their social network is constricted over time as a result of several factors. First, families themselves may be embarrassed by their ill relative's behavior:

> where she [the patient's sister] suffered was either she didn't want to bring her friends here or her friends didn't want to come because of him kind of taking over. . . . They didn't want to come because they didn't know what would happen. . . . I think it was the crudeness. When he is sick, his language changes, his appearance, his habits, they're all so gross. (Bernheim et al., 1982, p. 190)

Not knowing what explanation to offer to guests and worrying about how guests might respond, families find it easier not to invite people in at all. After a while, this results in fewer invitations to go out. If the ill family member is unpredictable or has poor self-care skills, the family may be afraid to leave him or her alone in order to spend some time away. Too embarrassed to hire a stranger to care for the ill member and unwilling to burden close family or friends who may know about the problem, they tend to take turns staying at home. Parents of mentally ill young adults, for example, rarely go out for an evening together, and most report that they have not had a vacation together in many years.

The stigma of mental illness also contributes to the family's isolation. Extended family and friends may be uneasy or even fearful about the ill person. They do not know what to say or how to be helpful to the family, so they frequently say nothing at all. Often, with the best of intentions, they participate in a conspiracy of silence.

> I noticed people wouldn't speak about her. . . . People would often ask about the family, and those who know about her would never ask how she was doing. . . . There was a point there when just a little interest or a word would have been helpful. . . . People don't know how to do it. (Bernheim et al., 1982, p. 79)

Another couple reported that they essentially lost all of their friends when their daughter, acutely psychotic, complained to all who would listen that her parents were poisoning her food. While these acquaintances no doubt knew that the charge was unfounded, they were frightened by the chaos in the family and kept their distance. The prevailing popular view that parents somehow cause mental illness in a child also contributed to the problem. This couple felt so hurt, alienated, and stigmatized that they were unable to repair these rifts when the acute situation resolved.

Thus, unlike other illnesses in which the family's pain is ameliorated, at least somewhat, by increased support and concern available through the social network, mental illness isolates and stigmatizes both the ill person and the family.

INABILITY TO PLAN

Mental illness also disrupts family life by interfering with the ability to plan for the future. Many of life's pleasures derive from expectations and plans we have for the future. But how can a family plan a christening party for a child whose father may not be released from the hospital on pass to come home, and if he is, may behave in a way that will be disruptive and embarrassing to all? How can a mother decide whether to take a job when her son may need her to take him to day program – if, that is, he agrees to go? How can a young adult arrive at a decision about going away from home to college when the extent of her mother's recovery from depression and the extent of her father's need for her help with the other children is unknown?

Finally, what Beale (1982) calls the "economy of coping" is profoundly affected by the presence of mental illness in the family. The expenditure of time and energy on issues related to the illness is massive. Family members often feel exhausted, with little energy left to invest in other potentially more satisfying relationships or rewarding activities.

Given the kinds of problems that mental illness in the family generates, it is not surprising to find that families commonly report markedly increased tension, risk of marital dissolution, and stress-related physical symptoms (Holden and Lewine, 1982; Hatfield, 1978). Of course, this situation is likely to extend over many years, with little if any respite. At the same time that the family members' adaptive capacities are being drained, they are constantly called upon to accommodate to and provide for the special needs of the ill member, as well as adjust to the changing lifestyles and needs of the well members as they go through successive developmental phases.

FAMILY TASKS

The family's task is easy to state but difficult to achieve. Simply put, the family must provide a highly structured, moderately stimulating, emotionally benign environment for its ill member while minimizing the inevitable stress and constriction in the lives of its well members. Given the intrapsychic and interpersonal chaos that mental illness in the family generates, this is a tall order, indeed. The surprise is not that families do not do it better, but that they do as well as they do. Creer and Wing (1975) report:

> We did *not* find . . . that relatives in general were tetchy and complaining. On the contrary, the majority were tolerant and accepting in the face of problems that most people would find distressing and many would regard as insupportable.

The vulnerability of persons with thought disorder to increased disorganization under conditions of overstimulation is well documented (e.g., see Heinrichs and Carpenter, 1983, and Bernheim and Lewine, 1979). Both life stresses (Vaughn and Leff, 1976; Goldberg et al., 1977) and family conflict (Brown, Birley, and Wing, 1972) intensify psychotic symptoms, need for medication, and relapse rate. On the other hand, deficit symptoms, including poor self-care and social behavior, lethargy, and lack of motivation, may be exacerbated by lack of stimulation (Wing and Brown, 1970). Thus, the family must learn to support, encourage and motivate its ill member without creating undue stress. Coping with a person who sleeps all day and wanders about at night, engaging their relative in household routine or therapeutic activities, and planning family events are examples of issues that commonly arise.

Of critical importance is learning to respect and provide for the ill relative's need for interpersonal distance. This is a common feature of schizophrenia and, to a lesser extent, of the affective disorders as well. Learning to read their relative's "signals" and to respond appropriately is necessary to achieving an optimal degree of social stimulation.

The nature of thought disorder also requires that the level of predictability and structure be higher in families with a chronically mentally ill member than in other families. While spontaneity adds zest to life, it often must be foregone in the service of the stability that routine provides. Thus, to complicate matters further, the sort of environment that is conducive to rehabilitation of the ill member may be boring and stressful for well family members. It may also take almost superhuman self-control to achieve. Primary caretakers, like parents or spouses, may be on the horns of a dilemma as they try to provide for the needs of both well and ill alike.

While the emotional tone of a family's interactions can have a significant impact on the ill relative's level of symptomatology and relapse risk, the presence of a mentally ill family member tends naturally to escalate conflict among all of the family members through a general increase in tension and through highlighting normal differences in opinion and style. Nonetheless, the family must work towards managing conflict in a noncritical, non-emotionally overinvolved way whenever possible. This paradox presents a major stumbling block to many families.

Finally, well family members must somehow provide for their own needs. Parents of a chronically ill child, for example, must attend to the quality of the marital relationship. They must ensure, to the extent that they are able, that their interactions are more than just discussions or arguments about issues related to the illness. They will need to give and get more than the usual amount of affection and support in the marital relationship if they are to function optimally under continuing stress. While most families make willing sacrifices for their ill relative, if they sacrifice too much they may lose their capacity for pleasure, useful activity, and human relatedness. As "burn out" is a risk for professionals who work with the chronically ill, families who are primary caretakers are at substantial risk too.

SUBTASKS

Of primary importance is the development of realistic expectations of the ill member with respect to personal, social, and occupational behavior. The family must take into account residual impairments and ongoing vulnerabilities as they attempt to sort out what their ill relative is and is not capable of achieving. Social withdrawal, idiosyncratic behaviors, poor grooming, aggression, and lack of motivation are examples of the kinds of residual problems that often accompany chronic mental illness even when acute symptoms are under control. Unrealistically high expectations can increase the risk of relapse, as well as family frustration and tension. On the other hand, unrealistically low expectations can prolong or deepen deficit symptoms, while increasing depression and helplessness within the family as a whole. Differences in expectations among family members must be resolved so that the ill member is protected from confusing demands and all members are spared increased conflict. Families themselves rate understanding appropriate expectations of patients as one of their most important goals (Hatfield, 1983).

A second, related goal involves setting priorities for behavior change and developing effective behavior change strategies. Given that the ill person is prone to confusion and disorganization in the face of conflicting or changing demands, the family must learn to focus on one thing at a time. Since he or she may also be particularly sensitive to criticism and perceived assaults on self-esteem, the family must learn how to encourage behavior change while minimizing conflict. Repeated failures are frustrating and draining for caretakers, as well as for the ill individual.

The family also has a significant role to play in monitoring the level of stress and symptoms in the ill member. Frequently family members are, or can learn to be, sensitive to what sorts of situations the ill member handles well or poorly. They can help their ill relative learn about the role of stress and modify the environment to minimize stress. This may include, for example, passing up horror films for light comedies or having friends over one at a time instead of in larger groups.

Families are often more attuned to prodromal signs of impending relapse than is the patient. They can often play a critical role as "early warning system" within the treatment network, provided that strategies for intervention can be developed.

Often the family will find it useful to take a role in encouraging the patient's compliance with treatment, through monitoring medication, making attendance at a day program a requirement for living at home, or other similar means. However, families find that this role must be handled most delicately lest it become an arena for defiance in the patient's struggle to become independent.

Another family task involves reducing the impact of the illness on healthy family members. Caretakers are at risk for exhaustion and emotional burnout. Attention must be paid to their own needs for support, socialization, recreation, and respite. Stress management strategies, both formal and informal, may be particularly valuable in this regard.

Finding a way for the siblings or children of the ill person to focus on their own developmental tasks (i.e., school, friends, hobbies) is a related issue. Both embarrassment about the ill member's behavior and heightened responsibilities within the family may contribute to isolation of these youngsters from their peers as well as diminution of energy and investment in out-of-home activities.

Finally, families must cope with the stigma associated

with mental illness. Lest the family become completely isolated from social support, some explanation for the chaos at home must be generated for extended family and friends. Again, different family members may have different ideas about how this issue should be handled. All family members will feel the inevitable pain that comes when they find themselves gradually isolated by those who are too fearful, confused or embarrassed to maintain contact with the family.

GOALS OF PROFESSIONAL INTERVENTION

The task of caring for the ill member over a long period of time is complex and draining. What sorts of professional interventions might ease the family's burden? A number of recent studies offer clues to what families want from mental health professionals (Hatfield, 1978, 1979; Kreisman, Simmons, and Joy, 1979; Yess, 1981; Creer and Wing, 1975; Holden and Lewine, 1982).

Information

High on the list is the need for information about the illness. While a case can be made that labeling may have certain negative effects (Doherty, 1975; Erickson, 1962), we share with families the belief that the advantages far outweigh the disadvantages. First, labeling the illness provides a cognitive framework within which to understand various treatment options and management techniques. Second, it decreases the tendency to perceive the individual as malicious or malingering. Third, it empowers families as concerned and educated members of the treatment network, rather than instigators or perpetrators of psychopathology. When they are expected to make informed choices in the interests of a relative with a specific, named illness, both helplessness and disabling guilt are decreased.

More than a label is necessary, however. Families need to know what symptoms are subsumed by the label—that is, what behaviors are within the patient's control and what are not. Understanding something about the etiology of the disorder – that is, what role biochemistry and environmental stress play in the development and maintenance of symptoms – helps them put unnecessary guilt and anger to rest, thereby liberating energy to focus on the present. Knowing something about prognosis will enable them to develop sensible expectations and plan for the future. Families also need to know about the effects, both positive and negative, of various therapeutic options, as they are often in a position to make treatment decisions for their ill relative. Finally, information about behaviors that may signal impending relapse will help them forestall needless hospitalization when possible.

Patients, of course, may also benefit substantially from the same kind of information. Compliance with medication and rehabilitation programs can be significantly enhanced by offering a sensible rationale to the individual (provided, of course, that the person is not actively psychotic when such explanations are offered). The chronically mentally ill can also learn to have more realistic expectations, feel less guilty about past symptomatic behavior, and modify their environment to minimize stress when they are provided with straightforward information about the disorder. Further, the "patient role," far from freeing the individual from any responsibility for his own health, offers clearly defined responsibilities to learn about the illness, make informed choices about treatment (at times when he or she is able), and cooperate with treatment which is instituted.

The provision of information is the first step towards developing a cooperative, consumer-oriented partnership with the ill person and the family. In such a relationship all of the participants have areas of expertise and areas of responsibility. While the relative power of the professional is diminished, the empowerment of the ill person and the family substantially contributes to a reduction of helplessness and resistance. Further, since dropout is related to lack of congruence between clients' and therapists' expectations (Heine and Grosman, 1960; Borghi, 1968), the development of a mutual understanding of the problem is a necessary feature of a successful rehabilitation program.

While some professionals are beginning to recognize the

value of this intervention (see, e.g., McFarlane, 1983), it is astonishing how little information is generally given to families with chronically mentally ill members. For example, Holden and Lewine (1982) report that one-third of the respondents in their survey of families of schizophrenic relatives were given no diagnostic information within two years of the family member's first breakdown. The majority (77 percent) of those who were given a diagnosis felt that its meaning was not adequately explained. While medication was prescribed for 95 percent of the ill individuals, only 53 percent of the families had been given any information about why it was being prescribed. Only 24 percent had been informed about the possibility and nature of side effects.

Information should flow from the family to the professional as well. Families frequently report having been frustrated in their attempts to share information with the treatment team. The emergence of prodromal symptoms, medication side effects, and anticipated stressful situations are examples of data to which families may have access. Thus, professionals must be prepared to receive as well as to offer information about the patient's illness and progress.

Help with problems in daily living

Along with an intellectual understanding of the illness, families may need and want help with management issues. Common questions involve how to respond to psychotic and deficit symptoms, foresee and manage crises, set limits on disturbing behavior, motivate and encourage the relative without causing too much stress, lower the level of criticism and conflict at home, increase structure in the ill relative's environment, plan for the relative's care when caretakers have died, respond to questions or withdrawal by extended family or friends, develop their own support network – and a host of related issues. In this context, direct discussion of these issues, as well as the provision of skills training in communication, assertiveness, problem-solving, and stress management, may be of great practical value.

*Education about the mental health
system*

The professional can also help by educating the family and patient about the complex mental health network. Acting as the family's advocate within this network may also be necessary. What are the credentials and competencies of various kinds of professionals? On what basis should one choose a doctor or therapist? What resources are available in the community for rehabilitation? What are the pros and cons of each for this particular individual? How much freedom do the family and patient have in choosing programs and professionals, and what are the geographic, economic, or other constraints? Is the ill person entitled to financial support? How does one go about applying for that? Fragmentation of services, lack of education about available options, inconsistent messages — these are frequent and well-founded complaints of families caught in the mental health system. The "case manager" concept has evolved, at least partially, to fill this gap in service delivery; in reality, however, this function frequently goes unassigned within the treatment team.

Contact with other families

Families report that coming together with others who have similar problems is tremendously valuable. As cocktail party discussions are not likely to touch upon mental illness in the family, it is generally up to the professional to provide these links for families. Interfamily networking not only reduces isolation and stigma, but also offers a nonthreatening supportive environment for families to learn new skills and approaches. It also provides an outlet for families' needs to be of service through advocacy and public information projects. Professionally led multifamily support groups, informational lectures offered to groups of families, and referral to local grass roots family support groups (like the National Alliance for the Mentally Ill and its local affiliates) all have their place. Whether these are provided sequentially or concurrently depends upon both the desires of families and pro-grammatic constraints. In our view, professionals who fail to facilitate these connections are passing up a valuable oppor-tunity to increase the coping skills, energy level, and perse-verance of the families with whom they work.

We have tried in this chapter to sensitize the reader to the often catastrophic effects of chronic mental illness on indi-vidual family members and family life in general. However, family members can do this job far better than we can. We suggest the interested professional read *Families in Pain* (Vine, 1982), *In A Darkness* (Wechsler, 1972) and *This Stran-ger My Son* (Wilson, 1968). Further, it is a good idea for pro-fessionals to attend several meetings of the closest National Alliance for the Mentally Ill (NAMI) affiliate (with their per-mission, of course) to listen to families in a situation where they are not personally involved as therapists (see Appendix B). In an agency a panel of family members might be invited to speak about their experiences. Finally, professionals should try to imagine themselves in such a family; better yet, they might arrange to spend an evening, a day, or a weekend as a family's guest. Only by listening to what families have to tell us and sharing their experiences can we bridge the gap created by our previous professional training, systemic power inequities, and mutual distrust.

We have drawn from surveys of families, as well as our own and others' professional experience, to outline a set of focal points for professional interventions. Such interven-tions must be collaborative, educative, and supportive. They are based on the premise that patients and their families are consumers of mental health service and are entitled to infor-mation which would allow them to make informed decisions. We believe that families are motivated by the best interests of their ill relative and are constantly juggling a host of con-flicting demands generated by the illness in their midst. These families have expertise which would be of value to professionals and vice versa. A detailed discussion of these interventions comprises the remainder of this book.

3

PSYCHOEDUCATION
AND THE FAMILY

Psychoeducational programs provide family members with
information about the patient's illness and treatment (Anderson, Hogarty, and Reiss 1980). In addition, they offer families
the opportunity to ask the professional how he or she views
and treats illness – for example, how he collaborates with the
family in caring for the patient or in structuring less stressful,
more constructive environments at home (Goldstein, 1984).
These programs recognize that in the era of deinstitutionalization, families once again must somehow cope with their
mentally ill relatives at home and need much more concrete
help from professionals than they have received in the past.
They accept the strong likelihood of biological causal factors
as well as the importance of the patient's environment in
determining the course of illness (McFarlane, 1983). In Chapter 1 we have already discussed two of the major reasons for
providing these programs: the high levels of burden experienced by families in caring for their ill relatives and families'
identified needs for more information and constructive advice
about patients' illness and treatment. In this chapter we
review a third impetus for these programs. This is the growing body of recent research into the impact of the family environment, in particular "expressed emotion," on the course
of chronic mental disorders. We then examine the major family psychoeducational programs that have developed during
the past ten years to improve patient outcome.

RATIONALE FOR A
PSYCHOEDUCATIONAL APPROACH

At the heart of the psychoeducational approach lie the compelling need expressed by families for more information and concrete advice and the growing evidence that the emotional climate of the family can have a definite impact, both positive and negative, on the patient's adjustment to his illness. In this discussion we will focus on schizophrenia because of the emphasis on this illness in available studies. It is likely that many of these findings hold for other chronic mental disorders, but at present there is little empirical evidence for or against this generalization to other illnesses.

Back in the 1950s, a British survey of outcomes among discharged chronic schizophrenic patients found that close emotional ties with families were associated with higher relapse rates (Brown, Carstairs, and Topping, 1958; Brown, 1959). Building upon this finding, these investigators (Brown, Birley, and Wing, 1972) developed specific measures of the family's emotional involvement with the patient, which they called "expressed emotion" (EE). Using a semi-structured interview technique, they recorded various negative emotional responses of the family and categorized them into subscales: critical comments, hostility, and emotional overinvolvement. Critical comments are remarks of clear resentment, disapproval, or dislike toward the patient; for example, "He's the world's most untidy person." Hostile comments extend this criticism to rejection of the person; for example, "He's a worthless slob." Emotional overinvolvement refers to a family member's unusual and excessive concern about the patient. This may be reflected in comments; for example, "A mother showed obvious and constant anxiety while describing such minor matters as her son's diet and the setting of his alarm clock . . . " (Brown et al., 1972, p. 243). Or it may be demonstrated by the family's actions; for example, a father actually quit his job so that he could spend more time caring for his schizophrenic son.

Using a composite index of these negatively expressed

emotions, the investigators found that 58 percent of patients with high EE relatives relapsed within nine months after discharge, compared to only 16 percent of those in low EE families. Furthermore, relapse rates for patients with less than 35 hours of face-to-face contact with their families did not differ between patients with high or low EE relatives (29 percent vs. 25 percent, respectively). However, for patients with more than 35 hours of weekly contact, the relapse rates were 79 percent in high EE families and only 12 percent in low EE families. The relationship of EE to relapse could not be explained by differences in patients' symptoms, behavior, or function, and thus the investigators concluded that family EE has a direct relationship to relapse.

Other investigators replicated and extended these findings in a study of schizophrenic and depressed patients (Vaughn and Leff, 1976). Nine-month relapse rates for schizophrenic patients with less than 35 hours of weekly contact with their families were 29 percent and 14 percent (not significantly different) for high EE and low EE families, respectively. In contrast, the relapse rate for patients with more frequent contact with high EE families was 57 percent, compared to no relapses for patients in frequent contact with low EE families. Antipsychotic medications added some protection against relapse among those patients in frequent contact with high EE families, reducing relapse rates from 92 percent among unmedicated patients to 53 percent among medicated patients. These relapse rates contrasted sharply with those of patients from low EE families, of whom 12 percent relapsed on medications and 15 percent relapsed on no medications. Of further interest in this study was the finding that depressed patients were even more vulnerable to relapse than schizophrenics in high EE families. Among the schizophrenic patients a threshold level of seven critical comments by the family during the interview was required to differentiate "high" from "low" EE families. Among depressed patients, this threshold dropped to two comments. Sixty-seven percent of depressed patients relapsed in families who made two or more critical comments, compared to a 22 percent relapse rate among depressed patients in families who made fewer than two critical comments during the interview. From these studies, the investigators propose that the negative effects of families with high EE on patient outcome may be modified by means of medications and reduced face-to-face family contact.

The validity of this relationship between high EE and relapse has been bolstered by a replication in California. Vaughn and associates (1984) repeated the Brown et al. studies and found relapse rates of 50–60 percent among schizophrenics with high EE relatives, compared to 9–17 percent among patients with low EE families. Preliminary results from other studies in this country have been comparable (Goldstein and Doane, 1982). The attractiveness of this line of inquiry is its integration of the strong evidence for biological vulnerabilities underlying schizophrenia (Henn and Nasrallah, 1982) with the evidence that environmental stress affects the course of the illness (Zubin and Spring, 1977). The emotional climate of the home and family members' feelings toward the patient can either increase or decrease the stress that the patient experiences. Thus, family members are not assumed to have caused the patient's illness but can play a major role in the patient's adaptation or maladaptation to it. Expressed emotion is an observable phenomenon without the assumption of any single cause. It may reflect both the emotionality that family members bring to bear on the patient, independent of the patient's illness, and the family members' responses to the patient's disturbing behaviors and symptoms, or some combination of these factors. High EE may be one of several normal response styles, but one which is ill suited to the special needs of the mentally ill (see also Chapter 6). Interpreted in this way, the concept of EE avoids the pitfall of biological versus environmental causation debates.

Despite the consistency of this association between family expressed emotion and relapse rates, this area of research is not without its critics. Hatfield (personal communication) has correctly pointed out that the literature tends to reduce families to either "good" (low EE) or "bad" (high EE) families and that this viewpoint is simplistic. It may not differ in a practical sense from the older "family as causal agent" theories. The implication remains that families may cause their relative to become ill, and the distinction between being the original cause of the patient's illness, that is, "schizophrenogenic," and contributing to relapse through communication of negative emotions can be lost. Professionals may still view the family as a negative factor in the patient's recovery, and this will affect their attitudes and actions toward the family. Recognizing that family stresses and coping patterns can enhance or detract from a patient's adjustment, Hatfield nonetheless urges a less judgmental and more empathic view of the family. Hence, although the research on family expressed emotion shows more promise than many previous lines of research into the family's role in the course and treatment of mental disorders, our understanding in this area remains immature. Caution must be exercised to avoid dressing up old, negative professional attitudes in new terms. Still, some helpful services for families have grown out of this line of inquiry, and these services fall within the psychoeducational realm for the most part.

SOME PSYCHOEDUCATIONAL FAMILY PROGRAMS

Recognizing that family attitudes toward the patient are determined by the family's beliefs about the patient's problem, by their past experiences in coping with the patient, and by their prior contacts with professionals, various groups of clinical investigators have set out to modify these attitudes. As we discuss elsewhere (Chapters 2, 7), critical and hostile family attitudes toward the patient can arise when the family believes the patient's problematic behaviors are simply a result of the patient's recalcitrance, laziness, or hostility, rather than related to his or her illness. These attitudes sharpen further when the family members find themselves caught between a seemingly unmanageable relative and an unsympathetic treatment system. In a similar vein, "emotional overinvolvement" may arise from the family's feelings of guilt and inadequacy. Behaviors and attitudes categorized by professionals as overinvolvement may be the family's attempts to correct perceived past wrongs or to "go that extra mile" for the patient, believing that if they just try harder the patient will get well. Hence, it is intuitively sensible to educate family members about the illness and treatment, to help them further develop their coping strategies, and to provide a more positive experience with mental health professionals. Here we review the major psychoeducational family programs that have appeared and the current evidence for their efficacy. These are also summarized in Table 4.

Leff and his colleagues in Britain (Leff et al., 1982; Berkowitz et al., 1981) have developed a program for families of schizophrenics consisting of educational sessions, multifamily relatives groups, and meetings with individual families and patients. Four brief educational talks are given to the families prior to the patient's discharge from the hospital. The talks cover the diagnosis, symptoms, etiology, course, and prognosis of schizophrenia (see also Chapter 5). This format emphasizes opportunities for relatives to ask questions and to discuss the material presented. As soon as possible after discharge a joint interview in the family's home is conducted by a psychologist and psychiatrist with both the patient and his relatives. The purposes of this are to identify areas of conflict and discuss ways of reducing the amount of contact between patient and family (especially in high EE families). These joint interviews at home are repeated as needed during a nine-month follow-up to help with conflicts as they develop and reinforce the goal of reducing contacts between patient and family. The relatives group, led by two therapists, meets every two weeks for an hour and a half and includes relatives from several families. Patients do not attend. This group provides mutual support for relatives, gives them a safe setting in which to express their feelings, encourages sharing of alternative solutions to various problems, and reviews or expands on information given in the educational talks. When possible, low EE and high EE relatives are placed in the same group, with the hope that the low EE relatives will function as models for the high EE relatives.

In their evaluation of this program, Leff et al. randomly assigned high EE relatives of schizophrenic patients to either the experimental program or a control treatment consisting of "routine clinical care." A total of 24 patients and their families were enrolled. Criteria for inclusion were a diagnosis of schizophrenia, at least 35 hours per week of face-to-face contact between the patient and relatives during the three months prior to hospitalization, and a parent or spouse with high EE. Nine-month relapse rates were 9 percent for the experimental group and 50 percent for the control group. The rates of critical comments by high EE relatives dropped significantly in association with the family intervention. All patients received neuroleptic medications in conjunction with the psychosocial treatments.

Goldstein and associates at UCLA (Goldstein and Kopeikin, 1981; Kopeikin, Marshall, and Goldstein, 1983) have evaluated a crisis-oriented family therapy approach in the aftercare of acute schizophrenics. In the face of high relapse rates among their schizophrenic patients during the first six weeks after hospital discharge, they developed a program of six weekly sessions of shared problem-solving for the patient and his family to reduce the stress and conflict characteristic of this post-hospitalization period. In essence, the family and patient face a crisis at discharge and need short-term help in successfully overcoming it. The therapy has four objectives: 1) to identify two or three current stressors, usually those that were associated with the recent psychotic relapse; 2) to develop strategies to avoid or cope with these stressors; 3) to get the family and patient to implement these coping strategies; and 4) to anticipate and plan for future stressful circumstances. The therapist takes a concrete, problem-focused approach. Antipsychotic medications are prescribed in conjunction with this family program.

In their evaluation of this program, the investigators randomly assigned 104 acute schizophrenic patients and families to one of four treatment conditions: family therapy with mod-

TABLE 4
Psychoeducational Family Programs*

1. A three-part intervention project:
   Ruth Berkowitz, Liz Kuipers, Rosemarie Eberlein Fries,
   Julian Leff
   Medical Research Council Social Psychiatry Unit, London

What:	a. Joint interview	b. Mental health education	c. Relative group
When:	a. ASAP post-discharge	b. Soon after— two sessions, four talks	c. Ongoing—1½ hrs.; a two-week interval
Who:	a. Patient Family Two therapists	b. Families Speakers	c. Families Two therapists

Objectives: Reducing patient–family contact and lowering EE for "high EE" families by providing encouragement, information/concepts, support, empathy, ventilation, focusing of communication.

2. A short-term crisis-oriented family program.
   Michael J. Goldstein, Hal S. Kopeikin
   Ventura Mental Health Center, Los Angeles, CA

   What: Six sessions of family crisis therapy

   When: During the six weeks following discharge from brief inpatient stays

   Who: Patient, family members, one therapist

   Objectives:

   a. To agree on two or three current, potentially stressful circumstances, especially precipitants to episode;

   b. To develop strategies to avoid/cope with stress;

   c. To get patients and families to implement these prevention/coping strategies;

   d. To anticipate and plan for future stressful experiences.

   "Six weeks of combined drug and crisis family therapy completely prevented rehospitalization and reduced symptomatology over a six-month period. Three to six years later, benefits of the brief treatments were still apparent."

*Adapted from Ryglewicz, 1983

TABLE 4 (*Continued*)

3. A home-based family intervention approach.
   Ian R. H. Falloon, Jeffrey L. Boyd, Christine W. McGill, John S. Strang, Howard B. Moss
   University of Southern California.

   What: Forty family therapy sessions, held at home during first nine months.

   When: When entering program: weekly sessions for first three months; biweekly sessions during next six months; monthly sessions during last fifteen months.

   Objectives: To pinpoint a small number of critical deficits in the family's communication and problem-solving behaviors and change them to bring about major improvements in family functioning. Change is effected through a behavioral, educational and supportive program, and 24-hour crisis intervention is provided. Superior compliance with treatment is noted, as well as reduced relapse rate.

4. A four-phase program in survival skills.
   Carol M. Anderson, Gerard Hogarty, Douglas J. Reiss
   Western Psychiatric Institute and Clinic of the University of Pittsburgh School of Medicine

   What: Four phases:
       a. Family sessions without patient
       b. Survival skills workshop
       c. Family sessions with patient
       d. Continued treatment or disengagement

   When: a. ASAP after hospitalization or episode
       b. One-day workshop, early in treatment
       c. ASAP upon stabilization, continuing six months to one year
       d. When functional goals achieved, option of intensive weekly family sessions or gradually decreasing maintenance sessions for a year or more

   Who: a. Family without patient, therapist
       b. Multiple families, leader/therapist
       c. Family with patient, therapist
       d. Same (sometimes parents or patient alone)

   Objectives:
   a. Connecting with family, establishing goals;
   b. Decreasing anxiety by providing information plus discussion of experience of episode;
   c. Enhancing boundaries, limit-setting, communication, patient responsibility

erate dose neuroleptic (fluphenazine enanthate 25 mg IM every two weeks), family therapy with low dose neuroleptic (fluphenazine enanthate 6.5 mg IM every two weeks), moderate dose neuroleptic without family therapy, and low dose neuroleptic without family therapy. None of the patients receiving family therapy plus moderate dose neuroleptic relapsed during a six-month follow-up, compared to 48 percent of the low dose neuroleptic, no family therapy group. Relapse rates among the moderate dose, no family therapy patients and the low dose, family therapy patients were approximately equivalent, in the range of 20 percent. They concluded that both the higher dose of medication and the crisis-oriented family therapy improved outcome and were most effective when used together.

In another Los Angeles program, Falloon and associates (1981, 1982, 1984) implemented a behavioral family program for schizophrenic outpatients and their families. Thirty-six patients were randomly assigned to either the behavioral family management program or individual therapy. In the behavioral family management program the family clinician meets with the family and patient in the home on a weekly basis for three months, a biweekly basis for the next six months, and then monthly. The first two sessions focus on educating the patient and family about the nature, course, and treatment of schizophrenia. Subsequent sessions consist of behavioral training in problem-solving and communication skills. (Chapter 6 explains these techniques.) Follow-up results comparing patients treated in the behavioral family program with those in individual therapy revealed significantly more favorable outcomes among the family-treated patients with regard to rates of clinical symptom exacerbation (6 percent vs. 44 percent) and hospital readmission rates (11 percent vs. 50 percent).

Perhaps the most extensive family psychoeducational program developed to date has been that of Anderson and associates in Pittsburgh (Anderson et al., 1980, Anderson, 1983). This program consists of four phases extending over many months. In Phase I the family clinician meets twice weekly with the family, beginning shortly after the schizophrenic patient is admitted to the hospital. These sessions typically exclude the patient and focus on the family's experience of the illness, eliciting their feelings, attitudes, and beliefs about the illness and identifying the specific types of problems they have encountered with the patient. The clinician becomes their ombudsman, making sure that their needs and concerns are addressed by the treatment team and keeping them informed about treatment decisions. The family clinician makes concrete suggestions about how the family can contribute to the treatment process, and by the end of this phase establishes a mutual agreement for continued work together, including specific, realistic goals covering at least the next year.

Phase II is a daylong, multiple-family educational workshop held early in the treatment and usually covering information about schizophrenia, medication, and management at home (see also Chapters 5–8). The therapist encourages family members to plan for their own needs as well as those of the patient. In addition, the multiple-family format allows sharing of experiences, problems, and potential coping strategies.

In Phase III the patient joins the family sessions after the acute symptoms of his illness have abated. Sessions are scheduled every two to three weeks over a six-to-twelve-month period. These sessions stress increasing the structure within the family's home (see Chapter 6), strengthening of interpersonal and intergenerational boundaries, and a closer relationship between the family and community support networks. To foster intergenerational boundaries, the parents are encouraged to spend more time alone together and to decrease their individual involvement with the patient. This phase also emphasizes a gradual resumption of responsibility by the patient. Simple, structured tasks are assigned to the patient with an overall goal of eventual attainment of his or her previous level of function. Finally, families improve their capacities to use community and treatment resources effectively and shore up their own support network. As Phase III draws to an end and the goals for effective functioning have been achieved as much as possible, the family has the option in Phase IV of either moving to more intensive weekly family therapy sessions or gradually disengaging from treatment through increasingly less frequent sessions. Evaluation results of this program are not yet available.

These four psychoeducational programs illustrate the major types of services that have been developed, although variations on the theme can be found (McFarlane, 1983; Snyder and Liberman, 1981). Most of the techniques that we describe in later chapters are consistent with various aspects of these programs. It is clear that these psychoeducational programs have shown superiority over no family intervention, but their efficacies relative to each other remain untested. Their specific mode of action remains unclear. We do not know if their advantage lies in their general supportive quality or in their capacity to effect specific behavioral and attitudinal changes in the family, such as reductions in expressed emotion, improved communication skills, and better-problem solving. Published evaluations have focused on patient outcomes rather than the changes that occurred in the family or the family members' satisfaction with treatment. Only the Leff study (Leff et al., 1982) measured expressed emotion before and after their program. They did find considerable reduction in EE.

Finally, the specific program components and characteristics critical to their effectiveness have not been identified. The programs of Falloon and Goldstein (Falloon et al., 1981; Goldstein et al., 1981) utilize only single family sessions, in contrast to those of Leff and Anderson (Leff et al., 1982; Anderson, 1983) where families are seen both individually and in multiple-family groups. Multiple-family groups offer opportunities for families to share experiences and coping strategies in a way that single family sessions do not. Besides being more cost-efficient (the same amount of therapist time benefits more families), this strategy may foster a greater sense of competence among families as they learn from their peers and realize that they know some things that can help others. On the other hand, individual family sessions permit a level of specificity and intensity in addressing the individual family's problems that may not be feasible in multiple-family groups. A current multi-site cooperative study of treatment for schizophrenia, funded by NIMH (1984), compares the Falloon program with monthly multifamily support groups and may help clarify this important issue.

Another distinction among these programs is whether or not the patient is included in the sessions. Leff and Anderson specifically exclude the patient from the educational and multiple-family group meetings so that families have an opportunity to freely discuss their feelings and focus on how they can cope with the patient. This can foster a greater sense of collaboration among the family members, particularly between parents, and avoids the awkward patterns of avoidance and "treading on egg shells" that can occur in family discussions with the patient present. The family may be more effective in agreeing on alternative solutions to its problems without the patient. While this may violate the "whole system" view of some therapists, it may be the most pragmatic way for the family to deal constructively with the problems posed by their ill relative. On the other hand, Falloon and Goldstein include the patient in the family sessions and Leff and Anderson include them in certain phases of their programs. Discussion and resolution of some problems require the presence of the patient, who must have a say in identifying certain aspects of the problem, proposing alternative solutions, and agreeing to whatever resolution is selected. We know of no studies that compare the effectiveness of psychoeducational programs that include patients with those that exclude them.

A third feature that differs across these programs is whether or not sessions are held in the family's home. All of Falloon's sessions are held there because this is the most natural and realistic setting for the family to try out new skills. Leff and his colleagues also hold some of their family sessions at the family's home. Obviously, this gives the clinician a much better feel for what is actually going on at home and is less inconvenient for families in terms of travel to clinics. It also gives greater assurance that the family will attend the session. The major disadvantage is the inconvenience for the clinician, who must expend additional time traveling and may have to compete with other distractions at the family's home, for example, TV sets playing in the next room, telephone calls, or spontaneous visits from neighbors. Again, we know of no systematic comparison of psychoeducational sessions in the home with those in the clinic.

We have a long way to go before we understand which program elements are critical to program effectiveness. In the meantime, families need our help and we must be willing to work with them using available psychoeducational techniques, integrating and selecting those program features that we feel best suit our particular patients, families, and settings. Family psychoeducational programs inform families about the patient's illness and treatment, create a collaborative atmosphere between family and professional, and encourage practical problem-solving and creation of a structured home environment to reduce stress. They seek to modify family members' attitudes and behaviors so that they may achieve a more satisfying life for everyone at home. Available programs differ considerably in their format, but all have shown distinct advantages over no family program. Further refinement of these programs awaits future research.

II

NUTS AND BOLTS

4

THE FAMILY IN CHAOS:
HANDLING THE
INITIAL CONTACT

Family members who are interviewed when their ill relative is hospitalized are seen at their worst, having undoubtedly experienced a major crisis which necessitated the hospitalization. Their energy, patience, and coping skills are thus at low ebb. Let us consider first the family whose relative is being treated for the first time. What are the feelings and expectations these family members bring with them to the first meeting with mental health professionals?

ENTERING THE SYSTEM

Acute episodes of psychosis rarely occur out of the blue. More typically, the ill family member has exhibited signs of distress or oddities of behavior for some time. Almost certainly months and perhaps even years of difficulty have preceded the first contact with the mental health system. For most of us, "mad" is the explanation of last resort. Families may have minimized symptomatic behavior at first, attributing it to a developmental phase in the case of a young adult or to a reaction to some environmental stress in the case of an older person. They may have attempted to provide support and reassurance, while seeking the counsel of other family members, friends, clergy and the family physician – all to no avail. They

may have been in conflict with each other and within themselves about how to handle the problem, and such conflict is,
of course, exacerbated as the ill person fails to improve.

Some families also label the behavior as "bad." If not con-
tinuously, then at least from time to time, they have perceived
their relative as lazy, stubborn, willful, thoughtless, and self-
ish. They have attempted to set limits, demand, coerce, bribe,
lecture, threaten, and punish their relative – also to no avail.
Since not all family members will share the perception of
"badness" at the same time, additional conflicts can be expected to have arisen around this issue. Further, as thoughts
that the person may be *ill* begin to develop, these normal
angry thoughts and behaviors provoke guilt and uncertainty.

Thus, family members who bring their relative to treatment are carrying heavy emotional baggage. They are confused about whether their relative is, in fact, ill. They feel guilty, not only about possibly having caused the problem in the
first place, but also about having mismanaged the problem,
having failed to intervene earlier, having been angry and inconsistent. They are frustrated and exhausted by continual
fruitless attempts to ameliorate the situation, embarrassed
by their inability to manage the problem without professional
intervention, heartbroken by the failure of their relative to
lead a happy, productive life, and fearful about the future.
They are often at odds with one another. One parent recalled:

> I remember Sarah [the patient's sister] putting up
> such a ruckus: "How could you leave your son in that
> place?" She was in high school then. I was really torn.
> I didn't know if I was doing right or wrong. I felt guil-
> ty. When Sarah got through with me, I thought, "My
> God, I can't do this to my son! I want to help him,
> but I don't know what to do." (Bernheim et al., 1982,
> p. 13)

They are almost always at odds with the ill person, who may
perceive no need for treatment and whose failed expectations
are typically laid at the family's door. It is small wonder that

families in this predicament appear disorganized and dys-functional.

INITIAL EXPECTATIONS

Families also bring with them expectations about treatment, colored by their own emotional needs and fears, as well as by their level of sophistication about mental health interventions. Usually, their knowledge about mental illness, its causes, and available treatments is gleaned from media presentations, which are frequently misleading and almost always inadequate. Many families hope for a quick and permanent cure. One father related:

> This was all new to us. When the doctor said he had
> to stay four or five days, I thought that was a long
> time, but I thought he'd be all healed up—you know,
> that he'd be a new man or something, a new kid.
> (Bernheim et al., 1982, p. 12)

Prepared by the medical model, these families expect that diagnostic tests will lead to a positive diagnosis with clear-cut treatment recommendations. They also expect their relative to resume or begin a normal life following treatment.

Imagine, for a moment, the frustration and confusion experienced by these families in the face of the vague, non-informative approach taken by many mental health professionals. Family members, seen solely as a source of intake information by the professional, may find themselves participating in a one-sided dialogue in which the professional asks all the questions, offering nothing in return. They may be told that their relative has experienced a "nervous breakdown," whatever that means, with little estimate of prognosis. They may be told that medication is being prescribed, or that a day treatment program is recommended, with little information about how these interventions can be expected to help. Their quest for information and guidance may be rebuffed and labeled (often covertly) as intrusive or overprotective.

Some families, burdened by stigma and guilt, may expect to be told "where we went wrong." When their sense of complicity is shared by the mental health professional, their expectations will indeed be met, but with a predictably negative outcome—they will become more deeply mired in the past, even less trusting of their motives and skills as parents or spouses, and paralyzed in their approach to the future.

THE "HERE WE GO AGAIN" FAMILIES

Since the chronically mentally ill, by definition, make numerous contacts with the mental health system and rarely stay with only one practitioner or one agency over the course of the illness, it is common to encounter families who have had several years of experience with both the illness and mental health workers. Frequently, previous contacts have been highly charged, negative experiences for the family.

> The sad reality is, I have been to approximately 33 psychiatrists in about 15 years and profited from their services in assessing how not to treat people, mentally ill or otherwise. (Hatfield, 1983, p. 54)

While the family's expectations for the ill member may have become more realistic over time, their expectations of professionals have changed as well—and rarely for the better. They may unreasonably blame past therapists for failing to cure their relative; however, they may also have had genuinely disrespectful or unhelpful contacts. In any case, the process of developing mutual expectations is complicated by their past history. They may be acutely sensitive to the imputation of blame. They may be wary of being forced into situations which are at variance with their judgment and wishes (including, for example, premature discharge to home). They may expect little sympathy for their plight and little credence paid to their own hard-won insights or suggestions. They may appear hostile, resistant, and demanding, or they may have a passive, "here-we-go-again" attitude.

The primary focus of beginning work with families should be on clarifying expectations and dispelling erroneous beliefs. The family's view of the professional as omniscient authority or moral judge must be replaced by the expectation of a working partnership in which neither party is to blame for the problem, both have some, albeit imperfect, expertise, and both are working towards common goals from a shared model of "madness." With experienced families, it is critically important to explore the nature and impact of their previous "treatment" and to spend extra time clarifying how this contact will be different.

THE BEGINNING

One way to begin, of course, is by setting family members at ease. A simple gesture like offering a cup of coffee or sitting away from, not behind, a desk can set the stage. It is important, in the initial contact, to take your time, to relax, to give the family the opportunity to relax. If you have allowed yourself too brief a period of time (less than an hour, say), if you glance at your watch a few times, or if you act as if seeing the family is a low priority item in your busy work schedule, the family will respond accordingly and a valuable opportunity will be lost.

We often begin by saying something like, "Gee, you folks have really been through the mill, haven't you?" As this often unleashes a torrent of thoughts and feelings (as well as tears), we take our time and allow the family members to tell us their story in their own way. Generally, we interrupt only to explore certain areas in more detail.

We want to know what information (or misinformation) the family has about the illness, its symptoms, etiology, treatment and prognosis. What is the source (or sources) of the information? What are the gaps in their knowledge? What questions or confusions do they have? This discussion allows us to estimate the family members' need and desire for basic information, their biases and preconceptions, and their level of sophistication. We are then in a position to choose, from among the educational resources that are available (see Appendix A for a partial list), those that are appropriate in each situation. While some people eagerly read and understand fairly sophisticated and lengthy books and technical articles, others will prefer pamphlets and other brief, non-technical handouts. Some will prefer to have the information presented verbally and some will find visual aids (a drawing of neurons, for example, or a visual illustration of a hypothetical "information filter") quite useful.

What aspects of the ill relative's behavior have been most problematic? What kinds of interventions or treatments have been tried in the past? Which worked well and which poorly? What situations appear to function as stressors for the ill relative? This discussion not only provides useful information to guide treatment decisions, but also acknowledges the family members' expertise and sets the expectation that what they have to say will be taken seriously. It also provokes the family to begin to specify behaviors that may later be targeted for change.

NORMALIZING

We also explore, mostly by empathic reflection, how family members have felt about themselves, each other, and outsiders (including professionals, acquaintances, police, social service agencies, etc.) over the course of the illness. How guilty do they feel? How angry do they feel? How alone do they feel? How hopeless (or unrealistically hopeful) do they feel? How much energy do they have available for assimilating new information and learning new coping skills? This strategy helps us make an initial assessment about how extensive our work with the family is likely to be and also allows us to let the family members know that their feelings (particularly their negative ones) are common among people in their predicament.

The conflicts that we see occurring between various members of the family regarding the appropriate way of understanding and caring for the ill person may be described as both normal and expectable. We point out that having a mentally ill person at home taxes everybody's emotional resources, aggravating other family conflicts and fostering both emotional distancing and angry outbursts. We remind them that this process occurs in families with any chronic illness. In this context we encourage family members to tell us (and thereby remind themselves) about their strengths, individually and as a family. Religious faith, sense of humor, interest in a hobby, and supportive behavior of one spouse toward the other are examples of behaviors that we take note of, aloud, as valuable resources upon which the family can draw. At this point in our contact with families we consciously avoid provoking or focusing on intrafamilial conflict. While later we may help the family identify and modify certain patterns of relating or communicating, our initial goal is to shore up areas of strength, combat helplessness, and empower the family.

Thus, while we may begin by taking a history, we do so only if the family chooses to begin that way, and with a focus very different from that of the standard psychosocial history. We are less concerned with chronological events in the patient's life then with emotional events in the family's life.

If the initial empathic remark does not elicit the family's story, we are likely to say something like:

> I'm sure you must have many questions and concerns
> about [your relative's] condition and what our plans
> are for [him/her]. For the next hour, I'm at your disposal. How can I be of help?

The family members are given the opportunity to set the agenda. They may begin by asking for advice about handling some problematic behavior. They may have questions about prognosis: "Will my husband ever be able to work?" "Should my daughter go back to school fulltime?" They may have questions about treatment: "Why does the medicine make him so tired?" "How long will she be in the hospital?" We attempt to answer these questions within the context of what we know about the illness, exploring, at the same time, how familiar or new the information appears to be for the family.

It is difficult to predict in advance what issues will be of primary importance to the family members. While their initial agenda is often different from what we had thought or hoped it would be, we have found that the development of trust proceeds much better when we address their issues rather than our own, at least initially. Therefore, we do not take a history at first, unless the family is eager to give it, nor do we give an educational lecture if the family has more immediate management concerns.

STYLISTIC ISSUES

Working with families of the chronically mentally ill requires adopting a style that is somewhat different from that generally used in outpatient treatment. Given that the family's adaptive defenses may be seriously weakened by prolonged stress, the counselor tends to be active, engaging, and structuring. In responding to the family's questions, there are several things we do *not* do. We do *not* turn the question back to the family, as in:

> Mrs. Smith, why don't you and your husband discuss together how to handle John's unwillingness to bathe and see what you can come up with?

We assume that they have already discussed it and have failed to find a workable plan. Otherwise, why would they be asking for our advice? This sort of response is understandably frustrating for families and constitutes one of the most common complaints about family therapy.

We do not insist that the family use a specific strategy. Rather, we say, "Do you think you might want to try . . . ?" or "How do you think it would go if you . . . ?" or "Some families have found it useful to. . . ." Acutely aware of the limitations of our own expertise and of psychiatric treatment, we are interested in developing a collegial, experimental, trial-

and-error approach to problems. We also do *not* hesitate to say, "I don't know the answer to that one, but my best guess at this point is. . . ." Families report having had many experiences in which they felt the therapist really didn't know what to do or how to answer, but acted as if the question were inappropriate or as if the family members should figure out how to solve a problem on their own.

Since the mental health maze poses a formidable challenge to families' ingenuity and perseverance, and since often they have neither the information nor the energy to make all of the needed inquiries and contacts, we are content to act as social worker, medical interpreter, or ombudsman as the need arises. In our experience, when families are asked to speak to the psychologist about vocational planning, to the nurse about medication, to the social worker about placement, and to the "primary therapist" about progress and prognosis, they are easily overwhelmed. In agencies where case managers exist, these are the professionals ideally suited to work with the family. In agencies without case managers, the family's counselor should be prepared to take an active role in shepherding the family through the system. This means more than just making an occasional referral. It means carrying information between the family and other members of the treatment team, scouting out programs and funding sources, and helping the family evaluate various options. In this respect, the role we have in mind is that of expert advocate.

PATIENT PRESENT OR PATIENT ABSENT?

Whether or not to include the ill relative in family sessions depends on a number of factors. Many family members prefer to be seen without the ill person, at least initially. Their recent interactions with each other may have been painful or even terrifying. This is particularly true if the ill person is being treated involuntarily at the family's request. Further, family members may have feelings, experiences, or concerns they wish to discuss, but fear that such a discussion may prove upsetting to their relative. They may also expect (often with good reason) that their relative will be disruptive, hostile, or embarrassing during the meeting. Given what we know about the effect of stress on psychotic symptomatology (in the case of the patient) and level of adaptation (of all family members), we would do well to override the family's intuitions only with great caution.

More often than might be expected, the ill person requests that he or she be allowed to be absent from initial family meetings. The ill person may expect (again, often with good reason) a replay of oft repeated criticisms or intrusive solicitousness. As the family members fear being embarrassed by the patient, he or she may fear being embarrassed by them. In addition, the individual may not wish to hear discussions about illness or symptoms. He may be at a point where acceptance of his illness and the possibility of future disability is difficult or impossible. The patient's preference, like the family's, should be carefully considered.

Sometimes the ill relative prefers to be present while the family requests his absence. If the patient is grossly or even moderately psychotic, or if hostile exchanges are likely, or if some members of the family are simply inhibited and unable to communicate freely in the presence of the patient, we try to convince the patient to allow us some time alone with the family. We reassure the patient that no confidences will be violated and that no information about diagnosis, prognosis, treatment, and other clinical matters will be given to the family that is not also available to the patient. This usually suffices.

What if the patient refuses to give permission for the counselor to contact the family? This poses a difficult dilemma. We must then weigh the patient's right to confidentiality against both the need for additional information from the family in order to provide adequate care, especially in acute situations, and the family's right to assistance. Confidentiality of information obtained from the patient must be respected in order to establish basic trust with the patient and to remain within the legal confines of professional care. However, if the family brings the patient to the hospital for admission, they are obviously aware of the patient's hospitalized status and at least some of the factors contributing to it. In fact, their input may be critical to decisions regarding hospitalization and immediate clinical interventions. There is no breach of the patient's confidentiality if someone on the treatment team talks to them about their perceptions and knowledge about the patient's illness and problems. Furthermore, confidentiality need not be violated in subsequent meetings in which the problems they face managing the patient's illness are discussed and resolutions considered. The therapist may need to inform the patient that his or her confidentiality will be respected, but that it is necessary to talk with the family.

In outpatient situations or when the family is unaware of the patient's treatment status, this approach may not be feasible or advisable. In such situations the family may be referred to a mental health professional who does not know the patient and cannot, therefore, violate confidentiality. This consultant could then provide education, advice and support to the family. The latter option could also be used when the patient refuses any and all communication with the family, as occasionally happens with paranoid or seriously estranged persons.

There are, of course, a number of circumstances in which including the ill person in family sessions may be highly desirable. Once the patient's reality contact and ability to concentrate and process information are adequately restored, he or she may well want and be able to make use of the same kind of information the family has requested. Giving the whole family the opportunity to clarify together the nature of the patient's symptoms, the role of nature vs. nurture, and reasonable short- and long-term expectations, for example, may prevent later misunderstandings.

In addition, some therapists (e.g., Kopeikin et al., 1983) have found that encouraging the patient to share with other family members the subjective experiences which occur during episodes of psychosis often increases the family's empathy and support. Likewise, the family members can discuss with the patient how they felt at various times and why they behaved as they did. Open conversation can diminish shame, while at the same time helping the family come to grips with the seriousness of the illness. Finally, the ill person's active participation is essential during sessions where behavioral contracting is being used and may be highly desirable when discussing expectations for behavior at home.

In general, we suggest a flexible, pragmatic approach allowing the ill person's presence in some sessions but not in others. To be considered are the wishes of each of the family members, the goals for the session, the predicted level of stress or conflict in the session, and the cognitive and emotional status of the patient. In some families, the patient's presence may be a stimulus for such highly charged, ambivalent feelings that most sessions should be held without him. With other families much can be gained if all members attend most sessions.

GOALS

By the end of the first or second session, we hope to have accomplished three general goals. First, we have communicated to the family our respect, concern, and wish to be helpful, not only because this will further the patient's treatment, but also because we recognize the family's rights and needs. Through supporting ventilation of feelings, dispelling erroneous expectations, attending to the content of family members' communications, allowing them to set the agenda, refusing to dodge or deflect questions, and adopting a relaxed pace and attitude, we hope to undo some of the iatrogenic effects which may have occurred in the past and develop a sense of mutual trust and cooperation. In terms of how power is distributed, the desired relationship resembles a stockbroker-client arrangement more closely than a doctor-patient one. Most family members have a reasonably good idea of what they want and need from us. We perceive ourselves to be the family's employee, called upon to provide certain information and advice. If we fail to perform adequately, we are liable to be replaced; this is an expression of the consumer's right, not of the patient's (or family's) "resistance." The family is encouraged to join with us in a trial-and-error approach to the problems in living they face. In short, we try to maintain a consumer orientation to the provision of service.

Our second major goal involves assessment. We want to know what information the family needs to function optimally. What do family members know about this illness in their midst? Do they know what behaviors are symptoms and what are not? Do they know about the role of stress in exacerbating symptoms? Do they know which situations are stressful for their relative and which are benign? Do they have realistic expectations for the future? Do they understand the role of medication and adjunct therapies? While we do not expect to fill in the gaps all at once, we want to have an idea about how best to bring this information to the family. We also assess how much help the family wants and needs in handling the day-to-day problems in living that invariably accompany chronic mental illness. How are they handling problematic behaviors? How are they managing the inevitable interpersonal conflicts at home? How are they coping with stigma? How well are they taking care of themselves and each other? Which of these areas are of concern to the family and which are not?

Our final goal for the initial sessions is to set an agenda for our future work with the family. For some families – bright, sophisticated, and experienced – this may involve no more than an occasional telephone call to check in and share perceptions about current status and future plans. For others, referral to the local family support group, in addition to occasional, informal professional contact, will suffice. Further options include provision of reading material and/or referral to family education courses or seminars, skill-building training in areas of communication, problem-solving, and stress management, time-limited regular counseling sessions to help the family achieve specific, mutually agreed-upon goals, and open-ended supportive counseling for long-term education and guidance.

The family participates actively in choosing from among these options. We explain each of the available services fully and offer our opinion as to which combination might best meet the family's needs. We also make clear that we see the plan as tentative and flexible. Family members are asked to let us know if, at some time in the future, they want something different from what is being provided. Of course, we also recognize individual differences among family members and may end up with a plan in which various parts of the "menu" are chosen by different relatives.

In discussing plans for getting together in the future, we also find out who else in the family might benefit from information and/or support. If we are seeing the parents of a mentally ill young adult, for example, we offer to see the well siblings, either alone or with the parents. If there are grandparents or other family members closely involved, we see them, as well. If there is a member of the clergy, guidance counselor, or best friend whom the patient and family would like included, we are happy to oblige. We try to encourage as broad a supportive network as possible so that the responsibility and stress of living with and caring for a chronically mentally ill individual can be shared.

5

EDUCATING
THE FAMILY

Families have consistently identified the lack of basic education about the nature, treatment, and prognosis of mental illness as a serious gap in the service delivery system. In this chapter we cover what ought to be included in an educational program for families. We use schizophrenia as a model, both because of its prevalence among families seeking help and because much is known (or can be reasonably surmised) about its etiology, pathophysiology, and course. Further, a coherent model, which links the presumed cognitive deficit that characterizes the illness to various suggested management strategies, is available. Sophisticated data and models for affective disorders also exist and will be covered, albeit briefly.

What is not presently available, although sorely needed, is a body of knowledge about serious, chronic character pathology, particularly borderline personality disorder. This diagnosis is being made with increasing frequency, and families of these patients suffer greatly due to the acting-out and impaired functioning associated with severe character pathology. However, there is little useful information or advice to offer them. The prevailing psychodynamic model is abstruse, arcane, and guilt-inducing, especially for mothers. Further, it provides nothing in the way of guidance about day-to-day management issues. While some researchers suspect that the borderline syndrome may, in fact, be biologically related to affective disorder (Gunderson and Elliott, 1985), a clear understanding of the etiology, biology, treatment, and course of this illness still eludes us. Thus, a psychoeducational program for families of character disordered patients will, of necessity, focus on pragmatic, nontheoretical management strategies similar to those covered in later chapters.

DIAGNOSIS: INFORMING THE PATIENT

Do we tell the patient that he or she has schizophrenia or affective disorder? There is no professional consensus on this issue (Green, 1984; Kondziela, 1984; Kundler, 1984; Garatt, 1985). On the negative side are concerns about misunderstanding, despair, and self-fulfilling prophecy. On the positive side there is the possibility of acceptance, understanding, and enhanced coping. Obviously, good timing and clinical judgment are indispensable, even if you believe, as we do, that the great majority of patients benefit from knowing the diagnosis and its implications. Patients who are grossly psychotic, paranoid, or intellectually impaired, for example, are unlikely to make good use of diagnostic information. Patients who exhibit denial and resistance should be approached gradually so as not to overwhelm the defenses and contribute to decompensation. Often these patients will accept having a "chemical imbalance" even though they will not accept having schizophrenia. In all cases, attention should be given to the misconceptions and stigmatization of these illnesses. In addition, the patient's requests for information (or avoidance thereof) ought to be respected. Here is how the beginning of an exploratory dialogue about diagnosis between a patient and a therapist might go:

THERAPIST: You seem to be feeling a lot better than you were last week.

PATIENT: Yes, I am. When can I go home?

THERAPIST: We think it would be well for you to stay another week to ten days until we get your medication stabilized. You've probably spent a lot of energy trying to figure out what happened to you, what the medicine is for, what the future holds. Now that we've had a chance to examine you we have a pretty good idea of what's wrong with you. Would you like to talk about some of that now?

PATIENT: I think taking drugs got me screwed up, don't you?

THERAPIST: Well, I think the drugs probably triggered a tendency you already had for your thoughts to get kind of mixed up. If it was purely a drug reaction, it wouldn't have lasted as long as it did. We think your symptoms come from a chemical imbalance in the brain that can get triggered by drugs and also by various other kinds of stress. It's a real illness, lots of other people have it, and the symptoms can be controlled by medication and by your learning as much as you can about managing stress in your life. This is a lot to take in all at once. Am I going too fast?

PATIENT: Is it like a brain tumor?

THERAPIST: No, a tumor is a growth of tissue. In your illness, the chemicals of the brain aren't working just right. Most people know the name of this illness, but very few people understand what it really means. The name is "schizophrenia."

PATIENT: You think I have a split personality?

THERAPIST: No, but that's what almost everybody thinks "schizophrenia" means. Split personality is a different illness – it's called a "dissociative reaction." What else do you think schizophrenia means?

PATIENT: Well, wasn't John Hinckley schizophrenic?

THERAPIST: Yes, he probably is. He had some pretty crazy ideas that led to his shooting the President. But very few people with schizophrenia are dangerous – that's another popular misconception. And if a schizophrenic person does threaten someone it's usually because he's scared.

PATIENT: Like when it took those four cops to get me into the car! Boy, I don't believe I did that!

THERAPIST: That's exactly right. You were scared to death because you thought they were going to take you to jail and leave you there, without a trial, and nobody would know where you were. Now that you're feeling better, you recognize that as a pretty strange idea, right?

PATIENT: Yeah, I was real paranoid.

THERAPIST: Right again. "Paranoid" means being afraid people are trying to get you or hurt you when they're really not. It's one of the most common symptoms of schizophrenia. We want you to learn all you can about schizophrenia because the more you know, the better able you'll be to cope with it. But you've got plenty of time — you can take it at your own pace. I'll give you a pamphlet to start you off, but is there anything you'd particularly like to ask me about right now?

In this example, the therapist introduces the notion of a chemical imbalance before using the label "schizophrenia." Were the patient more resistant to the illness model, more work would have been needed before the introduction of the label would have had potential value. Also, the therapist carefully reviews the patient's own ideas about schizophrenia and encourages the patient to use examples from his own history to enrich his understanding of the illness.

Why, one might ask, use a pejorative and stigmatizing label like "schizophrenia" when simply introducing the illness concept might be all that's necessary? First, as intelligent creatures, we humans use labels to organize data and decrease anxiety. A named illness is an understood illness (at least to some extent). Second, we prefer to actively and carefully dispel erroneous ideas rather than risk having the patient hear (or overhear) the diagnosis with inadequate explanation. Third, if the patient is to profit from reading and other educational aids, a diagnosis is essential.

It may be that certain patients are more likely to be hurt than helped by learning their diagnosis, although we think the number for whom this is true is very small. However, for families, information and education are imperative. Often family members must make treatment decisions for their impaired relative. The situation is in some ways analogous to that of a cancer patient, whose doctor and family share information with each other and decide together how much, when, and by whom the patient should be told. While forcing information on a hostile, resistant family makes little sense, we can think of no situation (barring patient refusal) in which avoiding the diagnosis with a family actively seeking information can be justified.

Handling Resistance

Sometimes patients and their families resist the diagnosis and its implications, particularly when information is offered early in the course of the illness. Grieving lost dreams, lowering expectations, giving up the goal of total normalcy, and accepting the need for long-term treatment are all tasks to be accomplished gradually, with large individual differences in the degree to which they are successfully mastered. Resistance is not an all-or-none phenomenon. The goal for the counselor is to find ways to address important rehabilitation issues without getting locked into fruitless battles. For example:

Lisa is a 28-year-old woman with a ten-year history of psychosis (variously diagnosed as paranoid schizophrenia, schizoaffective disorder, and bipolar illness, mixed) including seven psychiatric hospitalizations. Through a trial-and-error process she has learned that taking medication keeps her thinking clear and prevents episodes of devastatingly bad reality-testing and judgment. With the help of weekly supportive counseling she has learned to increase her dosage when she is premenstrual, when she experiences ideas of reference, and when she is facing external stress. She has also learned to make changes one at a time (for example, staying at home as she begins a new job rather than moving out immediately). She has developed a multitude of small but important coping strategies, like eating a few crackers while driving home from work so she won't be hungry, grouchy, and short-tempered with her parents before dinner.

Lisa has come to understand that she experienced certain failures because she was ill, rather than dumb, lazy, or bad. At the same time, she wants no part of reading about or talking about her illness by name, or of associating with other "ex-patients." She finds it anxiety-provoking, demeaning, and feels she knows what she needs to know to stay well.

Lisa's parents, on the other hand, have profited greatly from reading about her illness and from joining a parents' support group. For example, they are now aware that her episodes of squandering money and similar judgment problems have been due to misperceptions of reality rather than a flaw in her character. Therefore, when she is otherwise asymptomatic they are no longer overprotective or intrusive around these issues. They have become much more supportive of her growing independence as they have become skilled at recognizing the presence (and, importantly, the absence) of psychotic symptoms.

Many patients who are resistant to the illness model are willing to talk about managing stress when it is framed appropriately. For example, one might say:

People respond to stress in different ways. Some people get headaches, some get ulcers, some get depressed. It seems like when you get stressed you get ideas that other people are talking about you and trying to hurt you. You can learn to use these thoughts as a clue that your body needs you to take things a little easier. Let's see if we can figure out together what sorts of situations are most likely to make you feel that way, OK?

Some patients are willing to take medication because it helps them sleep, while resisting the notion that it also clears disordered thinking. In these cases, we help them become expert at monitoring their sleeping patterns and titrating doses accordingly. Since sleep disturbance and psychotic symptoms frequently coincide, we reach the same goal by an alternate route.

Another approach is to help the person (and the family) develop ways to test their hypotheses and yours about the nature of the problem. One might, for example, agree to take a patient off medication, even at the risk of decompensation, while alerting the patient about what signs and symptoms to look for. In this way a person who might otherwise stop taking medication suddenly and secretly can be convinced to decrease gradually while learning important self-monitoring skills.

Denial and resistance are natural defenses against what amounts to a psychic catastrophe. These defenses must be treated with care and respect. They will be given up only when the ill person and the family have found acceptable alternatives. At the same time, it is frustrating, draining, and occasionally infuriating to watch helplessly while patients discontinue medication against advice (again), or to stand by while families remove patients from treatment to pursue some new miracle cure, only to return when the situation gets out of control. Developing an empathic understanding of the patient's and family's plight, consulting (and mourning) with colleagues, and developing a farsighted view of the process of gaining insight will help the professional retain the strength and energy to stay involved and available. Just as change in the patient's clinical status is possible, although often slower than the family would like, so change in the level of insight and acceptance is possible, although slower than the counselor would like. The therapist who is committed to working through these defenses over a long period of time, which may well include several relapses, and who persists in helping clients learn from their experiences is in the best position to provide meaningful education and assistance.

Uncertain Diagnosis

What should we do when the diagnosis is uncertain, as in the case of a first acute psychotic episode or a psychosis with both paranoid and manic features? In this situation, we suggest that the professional offer something like a probability statement, along with some idea of how the issue will be resolved. For example:

> We're not certain yet whether John's symptoms reflect a one-time-only kind of breakdown or whether he has a predisposition for this kind of problem to recur from time to time. Given that these illnesses tend to run in families, and John's uncle had similar problems, we think the chances that this will just go away with no leftover problems at all is only about 20 or 30 percent. Once we get him stable, we'll gradually withdraw the medication and watch carefully to see whether his symptoms return. If he does begin to have difficulty again, it will probably happen within about six months and then we'll know he has the more long-term problem. In the meantime, we'll help you and John learn what to look for in terms of symptoms, and we'll help you plan getting him back into the swing of things gradually.

In this example, the clinician might go on to use the word "schizophrenia" if the ensuing conversation seemed to call for it, or choose to wait until the diagnosis is more certain if the family does not press for a label. Using a label does not require diagnostic certainty. It requires reasonable care in ensuring that the patient and family understand the alternative possibilities and how a differential diagnosis will be established.

Explaining the Diagnosis

Obviously, giving a label alone is not sufficient. Most patients, for example, think that the label "cancer" is equivalent to a death sentence. They need additional education if they are to remain hopeful and cooperative about treatment. Likewise, "schizophrenia" is embedded in myths and misconceptions. Attention must be paid to what schizophrenia is *not*, as well as to what it is. Specifically, we explain that schizophrenia does not mean "split personality," that schizophrenics are not necessarily dangerous, and that they do not generally require prolonged hospitalization. Schizophrenia is not equivalent to unremitting, totally debilitating insanity. The debunking of myths is best done by finding out what the family members know (or think they know) about the illness, rather than delivering a general lecture that may or may not target family concerns. However, this work can easily be done in groups, as long as people feel free to ask questions and clarify misunderstandings about the material presented.

We consider the "illness" concept to be the cornerstone of an explanation of any of the psychoses. Not only does it fit the available data, but it also defines roles and responsibilities for the patient and family. While neither patient nor family members are implicated in causing the problem, both are expected to work towards the patient's recovery. Nor do we consider framing the problem within a medical model to be antithetical to a strong consumer orientation, in which the professional offers expert advice and outlines options which the client/patient and family then evaluate so as to make informed choices.

We describe schizophrenia as a physical illness which affects a person's thinking, feelings, and behavior. We describe (and illustrate visually) basic brain biochemistry (neurons and neurotransmitters), using the dopamine hypothesis (Meltzer and Stahl, 1976; Andreasen, 1984) as an example of the sort of model that will eventually explain schizophrenia (substituting the norepinephrine model when discussing the affective disorders).

Minimally, the family should understand that the brain is composed of a series of "on-off switches" (neurons) that are connected to one another in complicated ways. While transmission of impulses along a neuron is electrical, transmission between neurons is a chemical process. The role and variety of neurotransmitters should be described, as well as the notion that an excess of dopamine in the brain may be at the root of at least some psychotic symptoms.

We use examples from the patient's own history or from autobiographical accounts of schizophrenia (e.g., MacDonald, 1960) to describe the breakdown in the brain of a "hypothetical filter" which normally allows us to attend selectively. In schizophrenia, the patient is acutely vulnerable to stimulus overload and related cognitive processing difficulties (see Bernheim and Lewine, 1979, for an extended discussion of these issues in lay language). Again, we are less interested in absolute truth than in providing a model that is easily comprehended and that structures the management advice we will provide later.

In this context, we spend a great deal of time describing thought disorder, including hallucinations, delusions, ideas of reference, and thought insertion or withdrawal, paying particular attention to the specific symptoms the ill family member displays. We describe affective and behavioral symptoms as responses to thought disorder. Withdrawal, for example, can be understood as the ill person's attempt to minimize sensory stimulation, while paranoia may be a way of explaining to oneself why perceptions and sensations are distorted and shifting.

We pay particular attention to describing such negative symptoms as withdrawal, lethargy, and anhedonia as the body's attempt to protect itself by "shutting down." These symptoms are often misinterpreted by the family as willfulness or laziness. When families are able to understand these behaviors as symptoms of the illness, they are better able to avoid exerting debilitating pressure to perform early in the recovery phase.

Patients also need to learn to take some distance from behaviors they engaged in while actively psychotic that are inconsistent with their value systems. When a patient says, "I put my family through so much," we respond, "The illness put you all through a lot—it was nobody's fault, not even yours." While working to reduce shame associated with past psychotic behavior, we try to enhance commitment to cooperating with treatment, so as to minimize the risk of future episodes. In other words, we communicate, "You're not responsible for what you did when you were thinking crazy, but you are responsible for trying to avoid getting in that state again by learning about your illness and cooperating with treatment."

We describe the illness as highly treatable but not curable. Drawing an analogy to diabetes, we describe controlling the symptoms with medication and learning to modulate stimulus input (stress) the way a diabetic learns to take insulin and modulate sugar intake. In this way, we raise the issue of chronicity without engendering helplessness or hopelessness. In addition, we provide a rationale for maintenance medication and for stress identification and management strategies to be taught at a later time. Hence, we offer a model that has heuristic value for the patient and family and stays reasonably close to research data. It is guilt-free, but outlines clear areas of responsibility for both patient and family.

QUESTIONS ABOUT ETIOLOGY

Almost always, the patient or another family member will ask what causes this illness or whether siblings or children of the ill person are at risk for getting it. Since data are, in fact, available regarding the genetic risk for both schizophrenia and bipolar disorder, we recommend some genetic counseling.

The point is illustrated by the story one man told us: He went with his prospective wife to her psychiatrist to inquire whether anything in her condition would bear upon their plan to marry and have children. They were told, "There's nothing to worry about." His wife, who was schizophrenic, later committed suicide, leaving him with four children, one of whom developed severe and chronic schizophrenia while another lived a marginal, schizoid life.

Paul Meehl's diathesis-stress model (1962) is helpful to families sorting out the nature-nurture problem. Within this model, one can have a strong genetic predisposition for the illness (the diathesis), such that the normal stresses of growing up and becoming independent are enough to trigger the illness. One can have a moderate predisposition so that significant stress (like loss of a loved one or vocational pressure) would be necessary to produce symptoms. Or, one can have no predisposition; that is, the person is essentially immune to schizophrenia no matter what the stress. We use the patient's own premorbid history, family history of mental illness, and description of current stresses to try to estimate, for the patient and family, the strength of the biological predisposition. This discussion also offers some clues to prognosis, which will be discussed below. We emphasize that while certain aspects of family life can be stressful (for all of us) from time to time, it is only one aspect of the patient's environment.

Professionals may be concerned that raising the issue of genetic transmission may inadvertently increase the family's burden of guilt. However, in our experience, while some families do react negatively to this information, most do not. Rather, they seem aware that they are not responsible for their genes and are relieved that their parenting styles and decisions are not at fault. They are, however, concerned about the possibility that other members of the family (the patient's siblings or children) may become ill.

It is true that the patient's children are at substantially increased risk (for schizophrenia, ten times greater than the general population). The patient should be aware of this so that informed choices about childbearing can be made. Siblings are also at increased risk and in this context we discuss age of risk and warning signals. If siblings are functioning well and have made successful steps towards individuation without incident, we try to reassure the family that the best predictor of future behavior is still past behavior. We also remind the family that statistically the large majority of siblings (approximately 90 percent) will remain well. The available data are even more positive with respect to children of siblings. Their risk is not substantially increased over the general population, with approximately two to three percent becoming ill (see Bernheim and Lewine, 1979, for a comprehensive discussion of these issues).

We explain to both the patient and the family that our knowledge of the genetics and biochemistry of mental illness is relatively new and still inexact. While the model is strongly supported by available data, family members will still encounter many people, including, perhaps, some professionals, who continue to believe that faulty parenting produces chronic mental illness. We tell them that such a view is outdated, although certain aspects of family communication can affect the patient's recovery insofar as recovering patients do best in a low-stimulus, low-stress environment. We encourage them to read the literature for themselves, educate their extended family and friends, and steer clear of professionals who blame the family or the patient for the illness.

EXPLAINING TREATMENT COMPONENTS

Since long-term medication is often a critical feature of successful rehabilitation, it is mandatory that this aspect of treatment be given careful attention in order to maximize compliance. Recall Holden and Lewine's (1982) report that while almost all of the patients in their survey were on medication, only 53 percent of the families were told why medication was prescribed and only 24 percent had been given any information about side effects.

The diathesis-stress model provides the basis for developing the patient's and family's understanding of treatment. We begin by explaining that antipsychotic medication blocks the transmission of dopamine, thereby reducing the level of spontaneous overactivity in certain parts of the brain. We use the term "antipsychotic" rather than "major tranquilizer" (a misnomer) or "neuroleptic" (incomprehensible to the lay person) because of its descriptive value. We also use the phrase "control of symptoms," drawing an analogy with insulin treatment of diabetes, to explain that medication does not provide a cure.

Families may be concerned about the potential for addiction when they hear that prolonged treatment will be required. We point out that the medicine works by correcting an imbalance rather than producing an artificial "high." We point out that antipsychotic medications are rarely, if ever, abused. We explain that symptoms may indeed return if medication is discontinued, not because the medication is addictive, but because the underlying deficiency in brain chemistry remains. Again, the insulin analogy comes in handy.

It is important that both the patient and the family understand that medication controls the active symptoms of thought disorder (hallucinations, delusions, uncontrolled violence) but has little, if any, positive effect on (and may, in fact, exacerbate) the negative symptoms (lethargy, withdrawal, lack of motivation). We also find it useful to emphasize benefits in *functioning* rather than in *feeling*. For patients whose illness is characterized by terrifying experiences, medication may indeed provide relief. For many others, who have experienced grandiose and highly pleasurable feelings when psychotic, medication brings an often unwelcome return to a dull and painful reality. When these patients are told to take medication so they will "feel better," they can hardly be expected to cooperate.

In this context a patient once remarked:

> You offer me an interesting choice. I can either feel dull and lifeless but function OK or I can feel terrific but spend the rest of my life in and out of the hospital.

This patient had been hospitalized seven times in fewer than three years, always as a result of medical noncompliance. When this painful reality was finally confronted head on (although the all-or-none way in which the patient perceived her choices was modified through further discussion), she was finally in a position to make an informed choice. As a result, her post-discharge compliance was dramatically improved.

Possible side effects of medicine should also be discussed with both patient and family. In particular, initial sedation, drying of mouth and nose, constipation, lowered blood pressure, akathisia, and Parkinsonian symptoms are sufficiently common and discomforting (not to mention frightening if unexpected) to warrant forewarning. Dystonia, which occurs in only about 3 percent of medicated patients (Ayd, 1961) is particularly frightening but both treatable and without long-term sequelae. Thus, the possibility of its occurrence should be mentioned. Finally, in light of recent evidence that tardive dyskinesia may be both more frequent than first thought and reversible if detected early, the family can be taught to function as an early warning system against this stigmatizing side effect.

There are several dozen antipsychotic medications, each with slightly different properties. In addition, there is wide variability in individual responsiveness to the same medication. Families can be helped to understand that finding the right medicine for their relative may be a trial-and-error process of many months' duration. Further, families can be most helpful in this process if they keep a written record of therapeutic and side effects of various medications at various doses. Generally, families are delighted to be offered a meaningful role and will comply faithfully with such a request. This task also helps to redefine the family's focus so that their natural tendency to watch the patient closely can be put to more efficient use.

It is extremely important to take as much time as is necessary to discuss medication initially and to be highly empathic and responsive to the patient's or family's complaints, concerns, or questions over the course of treatment. Of particular concern is the seductive pull of various "miracle cures," including orthomolecular therapy, special diets, and fasts. The attraction of these "cures" is understandable in view of the frustration and disillusionment that standard treatment frequently offers. We have found that disdainful dismissal of these procedures rarely dissuades families. Rather, the family will be more cooperative if the clinician carefully reviews the research findings, or suggests that untested procedures might best be reserved for situations in which standard treatments have failed, or agrees to incorporate some sensible aspects of the procedure in question into the treatment plan.

Maintaining a cooperative, nondefensive attitude increases trust and decreases frustration. Often, the family members need only a chance to ventilate (again) their sadness that their relative is so ill and that progress is so slow.

Medication is rarely the sum total of treatment. Programs which increase social skills, occupational functioning, and activities of daily living, as well as stress identification and management techniques and supportive psychotherapy, all play a role in rehabilitation. We help families understand that even after overt signs of thought disorder have receded, more subtle disturbances in concentration, motivation, and self-esteem may remain. Particularly if the patient has been ill for some time in young adulthood, important developmental experiences (such as dating or part-time work experiences) may have been missed. As a result the young person, while not psychotic, may be immature or inexperienced. Further, the illness assaults self-esteem, leaving the patient tentative and uncertain at best. We remind the patient and family that stress is implicated in risk of relapse, and we describe psychosocial treatments in terms of their stress-reducing potential.

THE ROLE OF STRESS

Patients and families have little direct control over the biochemical aspects of the illness beyond choices about medication compliance. However, they have potentially enormous control over certain sources of environmental stress. Here is where their energy can be used to best effect. Using the stimulus overload model of schizophrenia, we identify those situations which are likely to be particularly problematic for the ill person. We suggest that the patient avoid becoming overstimulated. For example, movies or television shows with lots of violence, quick action, or complicated plots can be passed up in favor of simpler, quieter programs. Small social gatherings can be favored over large parties. Working alone or with a small group of people may be preferred over work in which social interaction plays a large part.

Emotional intensity seems to be particularly hard for the

schizophrenic person to handle. In fact, a clear and comprehensive understanding of this issue provides the motivation for the family to explore ways to decrease the emotional "decibel level" at home. Further, positive as well as negative emotionality can be stressful, as illustrated by the following insightful remark offered by a 32-year-old woman with a 12-year history of schizophrenia:

> I don't think it's good for me to be in love. I can't take the highs and lows. I've learned over the years that I need a relationship with a lot of predictability, where I know what to expect and what's expected of me. If I have to give up some of the great feelings, well, it's worth it.

For this woman, as for others like her, a certain emotional reserve, a need for interpersonal distance, serves as a protective shield which should be left essentially undisturbed.

People with chronic mental illness seem particularly stressed by real or perceived assaults on self-esteem. Since the illness itself represents a massive assault on competence and since the course of the illness is often unpredictable, leaving the person vulnerable to relapse at any time, the patient's self-concept is understandably fragile. Minor criticisms, expressed either verbally or nonverbally, tend to have a disorganizing effect. Family members who understand their relative's sensitivity as a natural accompaniment to the illness are in a better position to modify their behavior accordingly than those who take it personally, claiming "he jumps down my throat no matter what I say."

Beginning a new job or going back to school represents a potential failure situation which should be approached with caution. It is not uncommon to find patients who stop their medicine and relapse rather than facing directly the feared situation.

Drug and alcohol abuse is another area of special concern. Many young patients seem drawn to a variety of street drugs. Perhaps in an attempt to self-medicate or to fit in with a peer group that does not stress achievement, they smoke marijuana, drink, and ingest amphetamines and hallucinogens, apparently indiscriminately. Not surprisingly, given the predisposition for cognitive dysfunction, many of these substances routinely exacerbate symptoms.

We find that framing our discussion of this problem in terms of drugs as a biochemical stressor engenders the least resistance. Families, of course, rarely need to be convinced, but patients may choose to test what we have told them against their own experience. Therefore, we explain, in concrete terms, the disturbance in functioning we expect to result and suggest ways in which the person might check whether our prediction is valid. We urge the patient to continue to discuss drug-taking behavior with us rather than deny drug use because then we can at least hope to engender some insight in the future. However, no patient will do this if the counselor's attitude is condemnatory or moralistic. An objective, educational approach works far better.

SIGNS OF RELAPSE

If patients and families learn to spot symptom exacerbation early, some relapses can be prevented through adjusting medication or by locating and reducing environmental stress. Others may be shortened in duration or lessened in intensity through early intervention.

Each patient has certain idiosyncratic changes associated with impending relapse. For one young woman, going on a diet is the tip-off. The father of a 20-year-old schizophrenic has come to recognize his son's asking for a haircut (when not psychotic he wears his hair in a ponytail) and refusing to wear his glasses as early warning signs. Another person experiences an increasing sense of being slighted or mistreated by neighbors before an acute episode. If the patient has a history of multiple relapses, it is useful to ask both the patient and the family to try to recall any behavioral or experiential precursors.

In addition, certain signs are suggestive of relapse for

almost all patients (Herz and Melville, 1980). Among these are changes in sleep, increased ideas of reference, paranoia, or grandiosity, and a change in activity level. These signs are pathognomonic for patients with bipolar illness as well as for those with schizophrenia. Spotting and reporting them early are important ways for the patient and family to participate in rehabilitation activities.

PROGNOSIS

Patients and families need guidance in setting both short- and long-term goals. Given the state of our knowledge, prognoses must be made tentatively, with an eye toward tempering optimism with a realistic assessment of the patient's present and predicted level of functioning. At the same time, the professional should avoid engendering undue pessimism and despair. In all cases, we should help the patient and family focus on realistic short-term goals rather than on the achievement of some ideal state in the far future. Nonetheless, some assessment of the probability of independent living, socialization, and vocational options should be offered. To be considered are 1) the patient's premorbid history, 2) response to medication, 3) level of insight and acceptance, and 4) availability of a long-term supportive environment.

In general, patients who had a good level of functioning before the illness, the onset of which occurred later rather than earlier, and acutely rather than insidiously, have a better prognosis. The more one can draw upon, in terms of adequate personality integration and successful negotiation of developmental tasks, the better. The risk with most of these "good premorbid" patients is that too much will be expected too soon, since the discrepancy between premorbid expectations and postmorbid level of functioning is great.

In particular, the often protracted state of lethargy, withdrawal, and impaired motivation that frequently follows an acute psychotic decompensation is difficult for families to comprehend and tolerate. Undue pressure to resume normal functioning during this period is often associated with relapse. We try to help families understand that these symptoms are part of the natural course of the illness and that a period of rest and recuperation is needed. Again, reference to the information overload model provides a framework within which the explanation fits comfortably. We encourage the ill family member to resume school or work on a part-time rather than fulltime basis and we suggest that responsibilities at home and in the community be resumed gradually. We also encourage families to tolerate their relative's spending substantial periods of time in bed or in solitary pursuits, at least initially, and to respect his need for privacy and quiet. Reframing these behaviors as "symptoms" rather than "laziness" reduces intrafamilial tension.

Of course, it is possible to take this approach too far, encouraging the family to expect nothing and the patient to achieve nothing. Helping the family to set clear short-term goals for increased functioning, based on a realistic appraisal of the patient's symptomatology, and to take pleasure in the achievement of these goals is an effective antidote to this potential problem.

Patients for whom medication provides substantial relief from psychotic symptoms have a better prognosis than those whose thought disorder remains active even when treated. Even though there is some variation in an individual's response to different antipsychotic medications, some assessment of medication responsiveness can be offered to the family relatively early. This should be done concretely, with reference to specific symptoms which remain and discussion of how these symptoms can be expected to impair various aspects of functioning. For example:

> John still has feelings that people are staring at him and thinking bad things about him. The medicine has helped to lessen these feelings so that he doesn't have them about his family and friends anymore, but he still seems to experience them when he's in a group of people he doesn't know, like in a restaurant or a store.

This might continue to improve slowly, but it's possible that he'll continue to be somewhat troubled by these ideas. So it may turn out that he'll need to have somebody he trusts with him when he's in those situations. Rather than expecting him to go places by himself, at least for the immediate future, the family may need to plan to have one person accompany him.

In addition, patients who experience troubling side effects may, quite naturally, find it hard to agree to a level of medication which would effectively suppress their symptoms. For these patients, too, the prognosis would be more guarded.

The ill person's ability to accept the illness and the need for treatment is an important prognostic indicator. Insight varies widely and affects medication compliance and decision-making. For some patients adequate insight is achieved early, for many others the process occurs gradually following several remissions and relapses, while others never come out of the stage of denial and rationalization. Working through this issue successfully depends not only upon the professional's investment and competence in educating the patient, but also upon the patient's personality structure. In addition, patients whose symptoms include feelings of grandiosity or other pleasurable experiences and ideas will, quite naturally, be less motivated to cooperate with treatment than those whose symptoms are frightening or painful. For the former, reality may be painfully dull, while for the latter treatment offers real relief from suffering.

For family members who want to know if their relative will ever be "normal" again, the generality and tentativeness of our prognoses will be less than satisfying. However, we try to offer some advice on structuring future expectations based upon our evaluation of the factors outlined above. As always, we are interested in helping the family understand the basis for our predictions, so that in time they will make educated predictions and appropriate expectations on their own.

We believe strongly, as do families we have known, that

information about the illness in their midst decreases helplessness and increases hopefulness. Data are beginning to accumulate that providing education of this nature may substantially decrease relapse rate in patients at risk (Falloon and Liberman, 1983). Further, education provides a role for the ill person and the family and decreases the power discrepancy between the helping professional and the persons being helped. It organizes perceptions and provides guidelines for effective decision-making.

Professionals have an obligation to develop the skills needed to communicate this information. These are essentially teaching skills rather than counseling skills, in that they include the ability to organize the material, present it clearly, respond effectively to questions, use instructional aids (reading materials, slides, films, etc) appropriately, and evaluate how well the information is being assimilated. In this chapter we have provided a basic outline for a brief, practical course for families and persons who suffer from chronic mental illness. In our view, such a course provides the framework for any real "helping" that follows.

6

CREATING A
SUPPORTIVE HOME

For most of us, home offers safety, basic sustenance, privacy, contact with and support from loved ones, and opportunities for relaxation and personal growth. Such an environment is particularly critical to the well-being of a mentally ill person, and indeed, formal treatment environments such as hospitals, day treatment centers, and residential care facilities attempt to replicate many of these characteristics of a supportive home. For a mentally ill person, normal life stresses, including those in the home, can bring on an exacerbation of symptoms. Consequently, families of the mentally ill relative at home face special problems. In order to maintain a safe, supportive, and therapeutic environment, they need to invest additional energy to control the levels of stress in the home.

Establishing structure within the home environment is critical to supporting the mentally ill relative. Families can achieve this by establishing clear expectations for the patient and themselves, communicating well with each other, and anticipating and resolving problems effectively. The family clinician can help families accomplish these tasks through direct advice, as well as through psychoeducational training to enhance the families' communication and problem-solving skills. In the first part of this chapter we discuss how families can reduce stress at home. In the second section, we review the techniques for training families in effective problem-solving and communication.

REDUCING STRESS

Establishing clear
expectations and structure

Mental illness disrupts the daily routines of patient and family and can create confusion in the home about who does (or does not) do what. The patient may assume irregular hours for sleeping or eating, withdraw from daily routines, or embark upon new projects due to mania or delusions. In response, other family members may alter their own daily schedules to accommodate the patient or find themselves embroiled in a power struggle. When such disruptions in home life arise, considerable stress occurs and it becomes necessary for the family to assert clear expectations and structure.

A 20-year-old man with chronic schizophrenia lives in an apartment in the basement of his parents' home. He goes to bed at 8 p.m. and arises at 4 a.m. at which time he plays his stereo and frequently awakens other family members. When his parents complain to him about this, he states that they keep him up by playing their TV set after 8 at night. They respond by not watching TV after 8, a decision which they find quite inconvenient.

A 27-year-old manic-depressive woman lives in her own apartment and is chronically hypomanic due to only partial response of her symptoms to lithium. She refuses all other medications. As a result of her hypomania, she causes frequent minor disruptions at her apartment house and the landlord has threatened to evict her if these continue. To help salvage this situation, the patient's mother stops at her apartment every day to monitor the patient and soothe the landlord. To do this, the mother has altered her work hours, which now extend into the early evening. Her later arrival at home means a later dinner hour for the rest of the family and has caused conflicts between her and her husband.

The first step in attaining structure at home is a regular daily schedule for the patient. Establishing regular hours for when the patient wakes up, eats meals, goes to bed at night, and completes basic tasks (e.g., making the bed, personal grooming and hygiene, small household chores) can help the psychotic or confused patient reorganize his thoughts and improve the depressed patient's self-esteem. For example, a 42-year-old man recovering from a major depressive episode commented how important it was to know that his family expected him to come to meals and how good it felt to fulfill their expectation, even when it was an effort for him. Such routines also help to prevent further loss of function in some patients, particularly withdrawn schizophrenic patients who otherwise become more and more isolated and nonparticipatory at home.

> A 24-year-old schizophrenic man recently returned home from the latest of several hospitalizations. Usually, after such a return, his parents would "keep clear" of him for several weeks, believing that he needed some "breathing space." He typically would withdraw into his room and relapse within six months. But this time, with the advice of their family counselor, the family established a routine for the patient, including taking the garbage out every morning. To their surprise the patient quickly accepted this routine and it became the focus of positive interaction for the entire family. They thanked him for his help, and he later was able to identify their willingness to rely on him as a major boost to his self-esteem. He has remained out of the hospital now for over a year.

A second step in establishing clear expectations is planning, so that there are few surprises (positive or negative) for the patient. Family plans for vacations, outings, visits by relatives or friends, or other activities should be discussed with the patient in advance. It is tempting sometimes for families not to discuss plans with the patient because they do not want to upset him unnecessarily or because they feel guilty about their plans (for example, a vacation without the patient). Sometimes they simply think it would be nice to surprise the patient (for example, a surprise birthday party with extended family). However, major psychiatric disorders such as schizophrenia, major affective disorder, and organic brain disorder are associated with impaired information processing and cognitive adaptation to change, which in turn lead to increased stress on the patient. Such unexpected events are usually upsetting to a patient recovering from a recent episode of illness, and it is best to share plans with the patient well ahead of time to allow him to collect his thoughts, provide input into the planning process, and decide how he wants to deal with the situation. This can involve plans for such minor events as going to the store as well as plans for such major events as an extended vacation away from home.

Third, the family needs specific plans to deal with problem behaviors related to the patient's illness. These plans should be developed in advance with the patient's collaboration, so that the patient knows what is expected of him, what is not acceptable to the family, and what consequences may occur in response to problem behaviors. Behavioral contracts with the patient can be quite effective. A behavioral contract specifies what is expected, when, how often, and what consequences will occur. The contract in Figure 1 was developed for a patient who had poor personal hygiene and was physically offensive to other family members at mealtimes. This contract was negotiated with the patient, who identified the incentives specified in the point system.

Behavioral contracts seldom work as easily as we might hope, however, and families will need to discuss and revise the contracts over time. If the patient is initially resistant to the behavioral change, the problem behavior may actually increase temporarily. In such cases families need reassurance to persevere in the implementation of the contract. The consequences must be ones to which the family is willing to adhere. Otherwise the patient learns that the contracts are not meaningful, and the family can be thrown into further distress. Usually modest consequences, such as withholding some of

Figure 1. CONTRACT

Goal: Bill will keep himself clean on a daily basis

	Shower in Morning	Brush Teeth in Morning	Put on Clean Underwear and Socks in Morning	Wash Hands Before Each Meal			Brush Teeth Before Bed
				Breakfast	Lunch	Dinner	
Points	5	4	5	3	3	3	4
Monday							
Tuesday							
Wednesday							
Thursday							
Friday							
Saturday							
Sunday							

60 points weekly = minimum to continue to live at home, eat meals with family, watch TV

80 points weekly = $3 allowance for personal expenses

120 points weekly = $3 allowance plus $5 for movies

_____
Bill's Signature

_____
Mom's Signature

_____
Dad's Signature

the patient's spending money, are palatable to families. However, families often must face more severe choices, such as telling the patient he cannot live at home if he fails to stay within the tolerable behavioral bounds. Many families find such consequences unacceptable. The family clinician should ascertain the family's "bottom line" before these contracts are developed. There are no easy answers to the difficult choices that arise when the patient opts to not cooperate with a behavioral program. Should the family expel the patient from the home, using external force such as the police or involuntary commitment, or should they somehow tolerate the patient's problem behavior? Behavioral programs can reduce the risk of facing such choices, but they cannot preclude it. Hence it pays for the family and clinician to know their limits ahead of time and to be sure that they have made plans and contingencies with which they can live.

Once the behavioral contract has been established, there needs to be a clear plan for monitoring completion of the contract behaviors. Did the patient really wash his hands? Who decides if the stereo is too loud? It helps to identify one person in the family who monitors this. Other family members may report on the patient's progress to this family member, and at times this person will need to make a final determination. He is a referee whose judgment must be accepted. If, after some time, the contract has not been effective, the plan is reexamined. Perhaps the expectations are too high or the contingencies are not rewarding for the patient. The goal is for both patient and family to succeed with the contract, so that they can move ahead to address other problems or goals. Approaches for dealing with some common behavioral problems are discussed in the next chapter.

Regular family meetings at home can provide an important structure through which the family discusses problems, goals, and plans. We advise some families to schedule a regular time for these. Some families establish mechanisms for developing agenda, such as an "idea" or "problem" box in the kitchen; each week the contents are reviewed and discussed. These meetings need not be formal and need not focus solely on problems. In fact, the family meeting works best if it flows comfortably within the family's schedule, for example, after the evening meal. At least some time is devoted to positive issues, such as a review of good things that happened during the past week or plans for special family activities. If a family has difficulty establishing this routine, the clinician can help by having them "practice" or model these sessions in the office.

Establishing effective lines of communication

Effective communication of expectations, feelings, dissatisfactions, hopes, limits, and plans is critical for a supportive home that reduces stress. Specific techniques for training families in effective communication are described later in this chapter. In addition, certain advice can be given to every family with a chronically mentally ill member:

1) *Be clear and specific* about what you want from the patient, what you want him to stop doing, and what limits and expectations exist. *Recommended*: "John, please stop playing your radio so loudly. It has to be turned down enough so that the rest of the family can't hear it if your bedroom door is closed. If you can't do that, we will have to forbid playing the radio after 10." *Not recommended*: "John, you're too noisy at night."
2) *Be calm.* "Mirroring" is a common phenomenon in communication. Speaking in a calm, controlled manner tends to have a calming effect and vice versa. Angry tirades about the patient's misbehavior often serve only to increase the patient's distress, disruptiveness, and symptoms.
3) *Be active.* Silence or sparsely informative communications tend to increase the patient's paranoia, delusional perceptions, sense of low self-esteem, withdrawal, or feelings of loss of control. *Psychotic patient speaking to her father*: "Dad, the telepathic waves in this room

are screwing with my mind. Can't you tell them to stop?" *Recommended response*: "Phyllis, I know that you must be feeling upset about something. I don't believe there are telepathic waves here, but I understand that you believe this. Let's try to figure out something that will help you feel more relaxed and less frightened." *Not recommended*: "Oh, let's not worry about such things now."

4) *Be brief*. While being active in communication, it is also important not to overwhelm the patient with information. Thought disordered patients may become more confused with this overload, manic patients may become increasingly energized, and depressed patients may become more withdrawn.

Family members can learn to be aware of the opportunities they have to reduce the patient's stress through effective communication and can be more supportive of each other at home in achieving this.

> The stepfather of a 19-year-old schizophrenic patient felt irritated and frustrated with his son's inactivity. He tended to "fly off the handle" at his son on weekends. Following the family clinician's advice, the family instituted regular family meetings at home and developed behavioral contracts to address the patient's inactivity. Both parents agreed that the father needed to tone down his angry outbursts at the son. Father was able to do this by keeping in mind the communication rules mentioned above, with reminders from his wife (not in the presence of the son) whenever he tended to revert back to loud, angry responses to his son.

Anticipating and resolving problems

The greatest risk to a supportive home environment is the family's (and patient's) sense that things are out of control and that crises cannot be handled. Stress levels increase dramatically when the family and patient feel like they are sitting on a bomb that may go off at any moment. Unfortunately, some families wait to deal with crises as they arise rather than anticipating them. Planning is the key.

The wife of a manic-depressive man knew that the early signs of impending manic episodes included decreased need for sleep and increased involvement in new projects. One day her husband bought a personal computer and began staying up late at night to work on it. Although she recognized the signs, she hesitated to mention these to her husband (because he would become irritable) or to anyone else (because she didn't want to betray his trust). Within a month, he had relapsed and was readmitted, having severely damaged the computer as he became increasingly agitated. Prior to subsequent discharge, the wife and patient worked out a written, stepwise plan of how the wife should deal with a recurrence, including:

1) Telling the patient when he begins to show signs of relapse (but not arguing with him about this.)
2) Asking him to call his therapist and to take his optional dose of trifluorperazine.
3) Calling the therapist herself, if the patient refuses, and arranging a visit to either the therapist's office or the local emergency room.
4) Arranging for her sister to be available to take care of their children if he becomes too unruly or has to go into the hospital.
5) Deciding beforehand that when she feels she can no longer manage him at home and that the above steps have not been effective, she will call the police to assist in transporting him to the hospital.

A 21-year-old schizophrenic man was hospitalized for his sixth admission in three years. His parents felt that they could no longer deal with him at home, because of their need to care for four younger children, and wanted the patient to move into a group home after discharge. During the previous hospitalization they had felt the same way, but had capitulated to their son's desire to return home. This time they were better prepared. They planned with the social worker how to tell their son that he could not return home and firmly supported each other on this issue. Anticipating an increase in their son's insistence on returning home as discharge approached and thus a potential crisis at the point of discharge, they developed a contract with him in which he would visit home one evening a week and one weekend each month. They presented this to him, and he agreed, although reluctantly. Nevertheless, this plan has enabled him to stay in the group home and has actually improved the quality of contacts between him and the rest of the family.

The major points with regard to planning for crises are:

1) That it be done when things are calm and in control, rather than at the peak of stress, when the entire family has less reserve energy to put into a thoughtful planning process.
2) To the extent possible, the plans are written so that the family members can refer to them at crisis points, knowing that the plans are their own and represent their best judgment of how to proceed.

FAMILY TRAINING IN PROBLEM-SOLVING AND COMMUNICATION

In this section we explain how the problem-solving and communication skills of families can be enhanced through family counseling. Before getting to specifics, we wish to emphasize that although family training in problem-solving and communication skills follows a structured behavioral paradigm, how this training is integrated into the counseling sessions must be left to the clinician's (and family's) judgment. This training does not need to be obsessively extensive, nor does it necessarily have to occur in the family's home. Furthermore, one can work on these skills with the entire family (including the patient) or with any subgroup of the family, depending on the circumstances. The important thing is for the family to be aware of the basics of problem-solving and effective communication so that these skills can be put to work for them.

Problem-solving

Certain steps are generic to all problem-solving approaches:

1) Define the problem.
2) Specify the goal for problem resolution.
3) Generate alternative solutions.
4) Weigh the pros and cons of each solution.
5) Select a solution.
6) Plan and implement the solution, including anticipation of various potential consequences.
7) Evaluate the results.
8) Continue or revise solution.
9) Don't be afraid to drop the solution that doesn't work and start again.

Obviously, few people actually go through all of these steps consciously in day-to-day circumstances. To do so would be excessively time-consuming and quickly overload most of us. The goal is not to create obsessive-compulsive disorders in families! Also, we generally assume that families of the mentally ill are no better or worse than other families in resolving their problems. It is just that their problems vis-à-vis a mentally ill relative may be more difficult, and failure to be well organized around problem resolution can carry more serious consequences. We are explicit about this from the outset.

Nearly all families will benefit from a review of these steps for problem-solving, and this can be done briefly in one session or in much greater detail over several sessions, depending upon the family needs. A review of problem-solving has at least three general effects, in addition to the specific information conveyed. First, it reminds the family that problems can be approached in an organized fashion. Second, it provides an opportunity for them to review how they deal with problems, what they do well and what they would like to change. Third, it usually increases their sense of control over the situation, or at the very least their hope that control can be achieved.

How much beyond a simple review of the problem-solving process should occur? When is it advisable to commit an extended amount of time to training the family in these steps, asking them to practice in the sessions and to complete problem-solving assignments at home? To make this decision, the family clinician must consider time constraints imposed by the family or other circumstances, the family members' current level of skills in problem-solving, their ability to tolerate structured sessions and homework, and their capacity to adapt their problem-solving style on their own or in conjunction with less intensive resources, for example, multiple-family support groups or readings. Most families do not need intensive retraining in problem-solving skills, and with a bit of support and encouragement they can make impressive strides. For example:

Bob and Sue, a middle-aged couple with a 29-year-old schizophrenic son, had had considerable problems with their son's aggressive behavior at home over the several years of his illness. Due to residual paranoia and grandiosity, he would frequently threaten his parents if they did not do exactly as he said and at times would strike his mother in this context. His older brother assumed the role of the "heavy," physically confronting and restraining his brother. This usually prevented further injury but produced considerable strain in relationships at home. His father felt guilty and ashamed that he had to rely on his other son for behavioral control, and the patient would verbally denigrate his father as "weak." When the other son moved away, the patient was chronically hospitalized because the parents felt they could no longer contain him at home. Weekend home visits would occur only when the brother was visiting.

A family clinician initiated supportive family counseling. The parents attended a one-day educational workshop on schizophrenia. Subsequently, the clinician discussed their past experiences in dealing with the patient's aggression, reviewed the basic steps of problem-solving, and reassured them that with some time and effort they could find a more satisfying way to handle the problem. Their goal was to have the patient visit home more regularly on weekends and eventually either return home or go to a group home.

One day, after the second family session, the patient threw a temper tantrum at the family clinician in the ward hallway, yelling obscenities, verbally threatening, and attracting much attention from other patients and staff. In the presence of both parents the family clinician remained calm, spoke clearly and directly to the patient, and succeeded in calming him without further incident. On the next weekend pass home, the patient began to throw a temper tantrum in the street in front of the family's home. The father remained calm, did not argue with the patient (as he usually did), and gave the patient the option of either remaining quietly at home or returning to the hospital. To the father's surprise, the patient opted to return to the hospital. (Usually the patient would stay at home, the family would cancel their planned activities, and they would all spend a stressful weekend shut in the house.) The father agreed to take him back and the patient quieted down and returned without incident.

Since this episode, the home visits have gone much more smoothly (and have occurred more often), the father feels more self-confident, and both father and son feel closer to each other.

This case illustrates how even a brief period of family education, review of problem-solving, and modeling by the clinician (in this case inadvertently in the ward hallway) can produce major changes in a family's capacity to deal with a problem. This family continues to use the family counseling sessions to plan weekends and deal with problems as they arise. The counselor has not engaged in highly structured problem-solving rehearsal or homework. This couple, like many others, utilizes the sessions to mobilize their considerable adaptive abilities in dealing with their son.

Other families require more structure and direction. This may include rehearsals of each of the problem-solving steps over a series of counseling sessions as well as homework assignments. The following progression of sessions is typical of this approach. First, the basic steps of problem-solving, as described above, are reviewed, and any questions the family has about these are answered. Next, they are asked to discuss how they deal with problems at home and to identify a list of problems they currently face. This open-ended discussion usually "breaks the ice," gets them to focus on solving problems in the sessions, clarifies for the family counselor how well they comprehend the problem-solving steps, and sets the direction for subsequent sessions by identifying key problems for resolution. During their discussions of past and current problem-solving patterns, it may be necessary to take some time to explore feelings of guilt or inadequacy. In most cases, it is sufficient to allow the family to express these feelings, to reassure them that they have done their best under the circumstances, and to reorient them to the task at hand, that is, to improve their success in dealing with current problems. If the family has difficulty getting started on these discussions, it may be useful to have them complete a "problem inventory." Such an inventory may be done individually or by the family members together as homework. It helps to have them rate the seriousness of each conflict or problem. Once the family completes the inventory, they select a problem on which to begin work, preferably one which they currently consider important, but solvable, and not excessively "loaded" with intense emotion.

For this first problem, it is best to have them go through the problem-solving steps in the session. This provides the clinician with the opportunity to further clarify the process and to identify potential pitfalls for the family. The major goal of this first problem-solving session is to give them a positive, successful experience so that they will continue on to more difficult issues. Some families will need help in selecting or defining the problem. They may want to take on the biggest, most critical problem first, for example, whether the patient should remain at home or how the patient can get a job. It is better to begin with smaller, short-term problems for which a workable solution is readily feasible.

A 52-year-old man was depressed and had not worked for one month. His wife, who was a housewife, was distressed about both his illness and their financial situation. He was receiving antidepressant therapy and individual psychotherapy, and his therapist felt that with some additional structure and encouragement at home he should be able to return to work soon. However, things did not proceed as quickly as hoped, and his wife and two teenage children began to feel more frantic about the family's situation. They expressed an increasing sense of urgency and helplessness. This seemed only to increase the patient's sense of guilt and failure. The family clinician chose to initiate problem-solving training to increase their sense of control. After reviewing the problem-solving process, the family (including the patient) chose a problem for rehearsal. They immediately selected the patient's unemployment, stating the problem as the patient's "lack of work," and the goal as "He will return to work." They then felt helpless and unable to proceed, expressing a mixture of anger and guilt.

The clinician helped them to reframe the problem. They reviewed the routine necessary for him to go to work, broke it down into smaller steps, and began to problem solve around these. The problem was redefined as, "Not getting up at a regular time in the morning." Their new goal was for the patient to begin to get up at his usual time on a working day, 6:45. Suddenly the feeling in the family session changed. This problem seemed more workable, and after brainstorming about alternative solutions, they came up with a plan. All family members set their alarms for 6:45. The son agreed to get up, start the coffee and begin cooking breakfast. The daughter set the table, and the patient's wife helped him wake up, get dressed, and come downstairs. For the first time in years, the family began having breakfasts together. The combination of medication, individual therapy, and the new family routine around breakfast quickly helped the patient get back on a regular daily schedule. Within three weeks, he returned to work.

This example illustrates the importance of properly framing problems, establishing realistic, short-term goals, and experiencing success. Once the family and patient succeed once, the problem-solving training proceeds much more smoothly. After these initial hurdles are behind the family, the clinician can usually devote more time in the sessions to helping them select the problems that they want to tackle, developing their homework assignment (i.e., to apply the problem-solving steps to this problem at home), and reviewing the results. The family begins to do more of the actual problem-solving work at home and uses the counseling sessions to review progress and to ask for the clinician's advice about specific issues as needed.

Communication skills

Effective communication remains a primary goal of family counseling. The emphasis has gradually shifted away from viewing family communication patterns as causal toward viewing them either as responses to an ill relative or as stressors that may contribute to illness relapse. As with problem-solving skills, our view is that families of the mentally ill are generally no better or worse at communicating than other families. They simply face a greater challenge. Living with a mentally ill person who communicates poorly or who behaves in a difficult way stresses the family's ability to communicate effectively. Failure to communicate effectively may have more serious consequences in these families, for example, relapse in the patient, violence, or failure to receive proper professional care.

As with problem-solving training, the amount of time invested in developing effective communication skills must be left to the judgment of the clinician and the family. We exercise care in initiating this process because some families may be put off by a focus on how they communicate (or fail to communicate) with each other. Indeed, most of us do not communicate all that effectively at times, and to place unrealistic expectations on these families may only contribute to their sense of failure and reluctance to talk about how they feel and what they want. The counselor should spend some time explaining to them that the patient may have difficulty expressing himself or understanding how others feel or what others want, and that such communication problems can lead to relapse. Reviewing these skills does not imply they have somehow caused their relative's mental illness or that they are less effective than other families in communicating. It may help to have them begin by discussing something as a group, so that the clinician can have a clearer picture of how they do communicate. One useful technique is to ask them to "plan a day" together. If it is feasible and they are willing, this session can be videotaped for later review together.

After this, the clinician can begin with a review of effective communication:

1) Express positive feelings.
2) Express negative feelings.
3) Make requests for behavior changes in others.
4) Listen actively.

Each of these is then explained in more detail. This usually requires more than one session. Some families pick up quickly on these principles and incorporate the ideas readily to improve their communications. Others will need repeated rehearsals in the counseling sessions and at home.

Expressing positive feelings is like motherhood and apple pie—easily endorsed in principle but not so easily achieved in reality. All of us can think of times when we wished we had told someone how much we liked what she had done or when we wished others had done so for us. It is amazing what a difference expressions of positive feelings can make in human relationships. Yet we often fail to do this because we are too embarrassed, in too much of a hurry, assume that the other person knows how we feel, or simply fail to note specifically what it is we like about what the other person has done. Effective expressions of positive feelings include:

1) A *positive verbal statement* about a behavior or event. For example, "John, I like it when you help your father rake the lawn." These are usually most effective when the person is doing or has just completed the behavior.
2) *Specificity* about what you like, rather than a global positive statement. For example, "I think you did a nice job cleaning the kitchen," rather than, "You are nice to have around the house."
3) *Genuineness.* Express the truth. Otherwise the recipient of the praise may perceive it as condescending, artificial, or even mocking.
4) *Nonverbal positive cues.* These may include physical closeness, friendly hand gestures, direct eye contact, or smiling.

Teaching these skills is an art. The clinician must help the family adapt this information to their own style. Rehearsing the expression of positive feelings may be dramatized a bit in the counseling sessions to help overcome the family members' reticence, but ultimately we want to increase their natural expression of positive feelings, not turn them into actors or salespersons.

Expressing negative feelings can be much more difficult for us than expressing positive ones. People typically say too much, too little, or hold in their negative feelings until they explode. Some suffer quietly and seldom speak up when they dislike what another person is doing, while others become angry and hostile, attacking the person rather than the action which is disliked. The most effective expressions of negative feelings:

1) *Are specific about what is not liked.*
2) *Express how it makes the speaker feel.* For example, "I get very nervous when you pace around the room," or "I am frightened when you raise your voice at me." These are distinguished from critical comments, such as, "You are awfully loud sometimes," or hostile comments, such as "You are a frightening person."
3) *Are genuine*, just as expressions of positive feelings must be.
4) *Include consistent nonverbal cues*, for example, direct eye contact, firmness of voice, and firm (but not threatening) hand gestures.

Expressions of negative feelings are usually linked to another component of effective communication, requests for positive change. Positive requests consist of:

1) *Specifying what is wanted.*
2) *Expressing how the requestor will feel* if the behavioral change occurs.
3) *Genuineness.*
4) *Use of consistent nonverbal cues* (good eye contact, pleasant facial expression, and warm tone of voice).

Example: "I get nervous when you pace around the room. It would help me to relax if you went for a walk when you

TABLE 5

Summary of Guidelines for Families to Promote Patient
Recovery and to Cope With a Mentally Ill Relative*

1. *Develop a long-range view of illness, treatment and recovery.* It can take a long time for a person with a serious mental disorder to recognize and accept the presence of the illness, to come to terms with its impact on his/her life, and to redirect his/her energies into pursuits that are both within reach and rewarding. In the meantime, your patience and your ability to keep a hopeful eye to an indefinite future is tremendously sustaining.
2. *Be consistent.* In managing a mentally ill family member, consistency is important.
3. *Have a simple, structured environment.* People with mental disorders have anxiety and are vulnerable to stress. They find it difficult to handle stimuli and are unable to sort things out. There should be predictable routines. The recovering patient is overstimulated by a "big event" such as a company dinner or holiday socializing.
4. *Slow down and quiet down.* This is a hard one for some high-gear people. Voices should be slow-paced and low-toned. Short sentences are best to reduce confusion.
5. *Learn the pattern of early warning signals.* Many patients with mental disorders eventually develop an ability to prevent illness episodes by paying attention to the signals of an impending relapse. Until then, your ability to sense those same signals is the best way to make sure that, should a relapse begin, it is mild and short.
6. *Accentuate the positive.* Excessive critical comments are to be avoided. Negativism is destructive in any family situation. The mentally ill are particularly vulnerable to comments that attack their self-esteem.
7. *Behavior problems.* Poor hygiene, arguing, and assaultive behavior can be altered somewhat in a gradual manner. Identify a behavior that is most annoying, focus on it, and see if you can get rid of it. Use leverage to see that your demand is met. There should be a penalty and consequences should be enforced. It is important to be firm. Limits on how much abnormal behavior is acceptable have to be set.
8. *Patient and stress.* The patient should be taught how to deal with stress. If a mentally ill person is in a public place such as a restaurant, and he/she feels stressed, perhaps he can excuse himself, go to the restroom, and "get himself together." He should be helped to deal with stress in a socially acceptable manner.

TABLE 5 (*continued*)

9. *Include the patient in life in ways that are not overstimulating.* Aside from not using medication and getting overstimulated, the greatest barrier to recovery is the loss of access to involvements that confirm the person's value to family and community. Your efforts to promote a sense of belonging, of being useful and cared about, are the sustaining forces until he/she reestablishes contacts in the wider community.

10. *Support the use of medication.* For many patients, medication is (as of 1985) the single most effective way we know to prevent the return of symptoms. Until the patient realizes this, your support for the use of medication is the best remedy to his/her natural wish to avoid it.

11. *Get your own life going again.* Every good family tends to stop living for a while when a loved one gets sick. That's fine when the loved one has a short-term illness. But when the illness is prolonged, the family eventually becomes exhausted. For your own well-being, it is essential that you pay careful attention to your own needs and your own interests. So get back to normal family routines. Pick up with friends again. If you don't have friends or leisure time activities, find some. And attend to the needs of other family members.

12. *Share your experiences with other families.* People who live with any illness firsthand in a family member know a great deal about coping with the countless problems of everyday life. As a general rule, families of the mentally ill know more about day-to-day life with the illness than professionals do. So listen to other families who are living with this illness. You will come away with new ideas and new skills.

13. *Become an advocate for the mentally ill.* Someday you'll get the hang of this. When you do, remember that there are many families who are still struggling to get to some kind of effective coping. With your accumulated experience, you can make a difference in their lives. So when the time comes, be prepared to be a resource.

*Adapted from McFarlane and Terkelsen, 1985, and Hatfield, 1984a feel like pacing." This includes both an expression of a negative feeling and a positive request.

Active listening completes the circuit of effective communication. The goals of active listening are to encourage expression of positive and negative feelings from the speaker, clarify what the speaker is saying, reduce conflicts and misunderstandings, and convey a sense of genuine interest which will enhance the speaker's confidence and self-esteem. Active listening includes:

1) *Consistent nonverbal cues*, such as good eye contact, leaning toward the speaker, occasional head nodding to acknowledge points.
2) *Asking questions to clarify points.*
3) *Repetition* of your understanding of what the speaker has said at the end.

Families of the mentally ill must expend additional energy to establish and maintain a supportive, structured home environment that keeps stress for the patient and other family members at a tolerable level. Establishing clear structure, reducing the unexpected, dealing directly with problem behaviors, reinforcing routines, and systematically planning to resolve problems are keys to achieving this goal. The family clinician can provide specific advice to families about how to structure their home environment and can work to help them solve problems and communicate more effectively.

7

REDUCING COMMON
BEHAVIORAL PROBLEMS

In the preceding chapter we described some generic principles and techniques for helping families establish a supportive, therapeutic environment at home and enhance their problem-solving and communication capabilities. Ideally, families will incorporate these techniques and proceed to identify and resolve problems as they arise, leaving the family clinician to play a facilitative role. Realistically, however, there are some problem behaviors commonly exhibited by patients that can cause considerable distress for families. The family clinician needs to anticipate with the family such behaviors as social withdrawal and passivity, suicidal thoughts and actions, aggression, carelessness, psychotic symptoms and behaviors, drug abuse, financial irresponsibility, noncompliance with treatment, panhandling, inappropriate sexual behavior, and institutionalized behaviors.

We recommend that the family clinician broach these problems even if the family does not. If there is time and the family members are actively identifying their concerns and problems, they usually will raise most of these themselves. However, if time does not permit or if the family does not initiate discussion, we will specifically inquire about each of these problems, usually by introducing them in an open-ended, nonjudgmental fashion. For example, "Families often ask me about their relative's potential for hurting himself or hurting others in the family. Do you have any concerns in this regard?" As an alternative, you may want to be more directive; for example, "Because families often ask me about the risk of suicide, I want to discuss this potential problem with you, even if it is not currently a concern." These types of problems are usually emotionally charged, stressful, and at times embarrassing for families. We have found that most families are relieved by the clinician's initiative in raising them and appreciative of the opportunity to ask questions and discuss them.

SOCIAL WITHDRAWAL AND PASSIVITY

I can understand that Sam is sick sometimes and hears voices, but even when the voices are gone and he's on medication, he just lays around the house. There's no excuse for that! A boy his age ought to get out and do some things. At least he ought to help around the house. Being sick is one thing. That I can accept. But his laziness has got to stop. He can't use his illness as an excuse to do nothing!

This expression of anger and frustration by the father of a 19-year-old schizophrenic man represents the distress commonly felt by families in response to the passivity, withdrawal, and lack of motivation displayed by many patients. These "negativistic" behaviors are, in our experience, the most common and troublesome problem behaviors that families encounter. These behaviors occur most often as part of schizophrenia, depression, and certain personality disorders. The counselor should start with some family education. The extent of it will vary depending on the diagnosis.

With schizophrenia, families need to know that so-called "negative" symptoms are a part of the syndrome, i.e., emotional blunting, lack of verbal spontaneity, lack of motivation, apathy, social isolation, and poor attention span. In addition, they need to know that these symptoms can be exacerbated by antipsychotic medications.

With depression, the family usually recognizes the negative behaviors as part of the patient's illness when the depression is acute and short-term. However, in prolonged depressions, particularly when not accompanied by more dramatic symptoms (such as suicidal thinking, delusions, and severe motor retardation), the patient's negativism can begin to wear on families. They may feel the patient is wallowing in self-pity, using it as an excuse to shirk responsibilities. The treatment of chronic depression requires a combination of psychological and pharmacologic interventions. From the standpoint of education about this illness, families need to understand that even after acute, severe depressions subside, some patients continue to have problems with motivation. This can be a sign that the depression is only partially resolved and that the patient's treatment needs to be continued or modified.

With personality disorders, family education poses more difficulties. According to *DSM-III*, some form of passivity or social withdrawal can be part of a variety of personality disorders, including schizoid, schizotypal, avoidant, dependent, and passive-aggressive types. These types are so varied and elicit such different responses that it is difficult to generalize about how to deal with them in educating families. One explanatory approach that we have used with limited success is as follows:

> Although your relative does not show some of the more overt signs of mental illness, such as seeing or hearing things that aren't there, or believing in strange ideas, we do think he suffers from a type of mental illness called a "personality disorder." Personality disorders are characterized by long-standing patterns of behavior, such as poor motivation or social withdrawal, that impair the person's ability to adapt and grow, and that usually are upsetting to others. We don't know the causes of these problems, although sometimes they are milder forms of a more serious disorder (e.g., schizoid personality and schizophrenia). Unfortunately, these problems usually do not respond to medication. To some extent the pa-

tient may be able to change these behaviors, but as
a family you may need to accept that they will not
change and decide how you want to deal with them.

Whatever the diagnosis, if the family understands that
passivity and social withdrawal can be part of the patient's
illness, that these negative symptoms can be adaptive for
some patients who experience stimulus overload, and that
with time these symptoms may respond, at least partially,
to a supportive, therapeutic home environment, they can proceed to develop strategies to cope with the patient's behaviors
at home.

Some patients typically withdraw to their room and avoid
interaction with family or visitors. This can be very distress-
ing for families if they expect the patient to participate in
regular family group activities or to visit with neighbors and
friends. The family may view it as rude when the patient does
not come to meals or leaves the livingroom to go to his bedroom when a visitor comes. In a situation in which the patient
is not interacting with others, the family must decide how
disruptive this is and what action needs to be taken. For example, some patients are unable to tolerate active conversation at meals, experiencing excessive anxiety and even an exacerbation of psychotic symptoms. Insisting that the patient
remain at the table during these mealtimes may only disrupt
the rest of the family's dinner and cause considerable distress
for everyone. At first it may be better for the patient either
to eat meals separately or to spend only part of the mealtime
at the table. Gradually the patient may be able to tolerate
and enjoy more interaction with other family members at
meals. Sometimes the family can change the format of the
activity to decrease the visibility of the patient's difficulty.
For example, they may serve a buffet rather than a sitdown
meal, thus allowing everyone, including the patient, the option of ending as needed. This, however, can go too far.

One family with a schizophrenic daughter who refused to come out of her room to eat soon found that

all of their plates were in her room. They would place a plate full of food outside of her door during meals. The patient would take the plate into her room, eat the food and refuse to return the plate. This patient eventually was rehospitalized when the family no longer had any plates in their kitchen. In this particular case, the patient was quite delusional and in need of medication before any other intervention by the family at home could have an impact. During the ensuing hospitalization, the family worked out a different way to deal with this problem. In reviewing the circumstances, the family reported that following her previous discharge, the patient had initially eaten meals with them, but gradually became more resistant to coming to the table. The parents felt she "needed space" and were reluctant to upset her by pushing her to come to meals. They failed to recognize her increasing withdrawal as a sign of impending relapse. Their new plan to deal with this was:

1) Patient will eat her meals at the table with the family.
2) After eating, she can excuse herself if necessary, rather than sit through the family's usual post-meal discussions.
3) If any member of the family feels the patient is again reverting to her previous level of withdrawal (i.e., missing meals more than once per week, leaving the table within ten minutes of arrival, or appearing distressed at the table), he must discuss this with the patient's mother, who in turn will discuss it with the patient. (This arrangement was devised by the family because the patient usually retained some rapport with the mother, even when overtly psychotic.)
4) The mother would contact the patient's psychiatrist if these signs of relapse appeared. By pri-

or agreement with the psychiatrist, the mother
would have the patient increase her daily antipsychotic drug dose.

5) Within one week, the patient would be seen by
her psychiatrist to evaluate her mental status
and medication dosage.

6) Under no circumstances would the family
revert to its prior pattern of bringing the patient's meals to her room.

At other times, when the patient's passivity is not due to
impending relapse, the family may need to apply additional
structure to the patient's time in order to decrease withdrawal. A simple daily schedule is a good way to structure the patient's day. This clarifies what is expected of him and helps
him remain involved to the level of his current ability. The
patient may be expected to be out of bed and have his room
cleaned by a certain time. He may also be expected to take
a shower or brush his teeth and to attend to meals, or at least
eat meals, on schedule with the rest of the family. These tasks
can be broken into smaller steps if the patient has difficulty
with them. Setting clear expectations and goals which the patient can attain has a dual benefit. It gets the patient involved,
and it provides a positive experience that helps to overcome
fear of failure and increase self-esteem. The techniques for
helping the family establish this structure and planned successes were described in the preceding chapter.

In the situation in which the patient secludes himself in
his room whenever company comes, it is important for the
family to be sensitive to the difficulties he may experience
in social interactions. Again, it may be far better to allow the
patient to take himself out of a situation that is stressful than
to insist that he remain at the risk of precipitating a family
argument or major disruption of the visit. This only produces
embarrassment for the family and the patient, not to mention
the visitors, and further alienates both the patient and the
family from friends and relatives. When a patient indicates
inability to tolerate or lack of desire to see visitors, we recom-

mend that the family respect this. With gentle encouragement and support, the patient may gradually be able to spend increasingly longer amounts of time socializing. The family may want to begin with small gatherings rather than large ones, in a familiar setting rather than away from home, and with trusted friends rather than strangers. This positive and tolerant approach to the patient's self-regulation of social interactions often proves more effective than does a rigid insistence that the patient "be polite" and remain in the room. It often helps if the family and patient have discussed beforehand how they want to handle these visits. Having an agreed-upon plan avoids embarrassing "negotiations" while the visitors stand by awkwardly.

SUICIDAL THOUGHTS AND BEHAVIORS

Most families recognize the need for immediate professional help when the patient is overtly suicidal. However, difficulties may arise when the patient's suicidal intentions are expressed in more subtle, ambiguous, or idiosyncratic fashions. Even when the potential for suicide is recognized, the family may need help to understand what they can do and to acknowledge that there are some things they simply cannot control. Whether or not a patient is currently at risk for suicide, it pays to review with the family some of the more common warning signals of suicidal intentions, including:

1) Feelings of worthlessness or hopelessness.
2) Preoccupation with morbid topics or death.
3) Withdrawal from previous activities or relationships.
4) Increased risk-taking behaviors (e.g., driving too fast, drinking heavily, playing with knives or guns).
5) Sudden brightening of mood or increased activity in someone who has been seriously depressed.
6) Putting one's affairs in order (e.g., writing a will, giving prized possessions to loved ones, saying goodbye to people).
7) Feelings of anguish or desperation.

8) Hallucinations that are highly critical of the patient or that command the patient to hurt himself.
9) Sleeplessness, loss of appetite, and other "vegetative" symptoms of depression.
10) A concrete plan for suicide.

After a review of these common warning signs, the family can discuss any patterns that they have observed in the patient prior to suicidal episodes. Sometimes the patient can be quite helpful in explaining to them what he notices about himself when he is suicidal. A careful review of the idiosyncratic behavioral patterns leading up to a suicide attempt can be especially useful for families of schizophrenic patients.

A young schizophrenic man returned to his home after a lengthy hospitalization. Despite treatment with antipsychotic medications, he remained delusional, although improved over his more acute state at the time of hospitalization. Because of his delusions, the patient continued to behave in a rather bizarre fashion at home, isolating himself in his room and being uncommunicative. After a month of this behavior, the patient began to throw family possessions into the garbage. The family viewed this as troublesome but did not discuss it with him in any detail because of his apparently fragile psychological state and their fears that he might become aggressive. One day he began throwing many of his prize possessions out of his bedroom window, stating that he no longer needed them. Confronted with this, the family finally brought the patient back to the hospital. It was only after his readmission that he displayed overtly suicidal behavior. In retrospect, throwing away his most cherished belongings was his psychotic way of telling his family that he did not have long to live. Voices were commanding him to kill himself. Fortunately in this case, the family responded to his "cry for help," even though they did not recognize that he was suicidal.

Having established with the family an enhanced recognition of suicide potential, the next step is to develop strategies to cope with the problem. They may need to limit the patient's access to guns, knives, medications, automobiles, and other potentially lethal implements. Certain patterns of family responses may only exacerbate the situation, and they need to recognize these. Attempts to argue the patient out of suicidal ideas may only increase the patient's insistence upon them. Angry responses can further erode the patient's sense of self-esteem and increase the patient's sense that the family would be better off if he were not around.

If the patient verbalizes suicidal intentions, it is critical that the family recognize the importance of prompt professional intervention. Beyond this, they may lend an empathic ear to the patient's suicidal concerns and be clear with the patient about the limits of their abilities to prevent his suicide. For example, in response to the patient's repeated statements that he feels like killing himself, the family member may respond:

> I know that you are hurting and that things need to change for you. We all love you very much, need you, and would feel very bad if you were to die. I am glad that you are able to tell me how bad you feel so that together we can get you some help. I'm concerned that we cannot stop you from hurting yourself if you are determined to do so, and we need to go see your doctor now to get some additional help.

As with other problem situations, the optimum time to decide what to do is not in the midst of the crisis. The family clinician can help the family develop a written plan of steps for dealing with the situation. Using the problem-solving techniques described in the previous chapter, the family members specify for themselves what they will do when the patient becomes suicidal. At what point will they institute certain restrictions, for example, preventing the patient's use of the family automobile or assigning one of them to be with the patient at all times? When will they seek outside help, and whom will they call? How will they get the patient to help? Will they call an ambulance or the police to transport the patient? The more these details are worked out beforehand, the easier it will be for the family to respond to the patient's need at the time and the less likely the risk of tragedy.

One young man with paranoid schizophrenia and obsessive-compulsive traits had repeatedly attempted to kill himself. After a period of observation in the hospital and review of the family's observations of these episodes at home, it became apparent that, prior to each attempt, the patient began drinking water compulsively. Once this pattern was identified, the family members felt more comfortable with their ability to predict the seemingly random attempts by the patient to harm himself. It was then possible to work out with them a series of contingency plans at home when the patient began to behave in this manner. These contingencies included upward adjustment of the patient's medication, immediate contact with the patient's therapist, and early intervention with short-term inpatient treatment. This carefully planned approach not only reduced the risk of the patient actually harming himself, but also increased the family's sense of control over the situation.

AGGRESSION

Although violence among the mentally ill is probably less common than thought by the general public, some patients in a fit of anger or psychosis do smash furniture or put their fists through walls. Others become aggressive toward a relative or threaten neighbors. Such behaviors by patients exact heavy tolls on families, in the form of injuries and physical destruction of property, as well as emotional drain (constantly living in fear that the patient may act out his/her aggressive impulses) and alienation from friends, other relatives, and neighbors. Our approach to help a family deal with aggression is basically the same as that for suicidal behaviors:

1) Review the common warning signs of impending aggression.
2) Review the patient's idiosyncratic patterns of aggression.
3) Identify why the patient is becoming aggressive.
4) Help the family develop concrete strategies for dealing with the patient's threats and violent behaviors.

Some of the signs of impending aggressive behaviors include increasing fearfulness, agitation, disorganization in thinking or behavior, suspiciousness, delusions that some threat to self exists, irritability, and argumentativeness. In recognizing these signs, the family and clinician must consider the reasons for the patient's aggression, since this will to some extent guide their planned responses. Patients may become aggressive in a variety of situations:

1) The damage or injury occurs as a result of attempts to restrain or subdue an agitated patient. In these circumstances the patient does not intend harm, but an injury occurs inadvertently in the process of physically restraining the patient; for example, a demented, elderly patient who is acutely disoriented, agitated, and flailing his arms inadvertently strikes his son who is attempting to get him to lie down.
2) The patient may misperceive a situation and feel that he is in imminent danger. The response is to strike out as a self-protective measure. Such a situation is most common among paranoid patients; for example, one patient struck his mother while he was suffering from a delusion that she was attempting to poison him.
3) The patient may be suffering from other psychotic symptoms which lead to an attempt to harm others or damage property; for example, a patient has auditory hallucinations that command him to kill his father.
4) The patient may purposely decide to try to hurt someone or damage property for nonpsychotic reasons. This may happen when the patient believes he has been wronged and seeks revenge, for example, retribution

against family members who decided to seek involuntary hospitalization for the patient.

In the first instance of the disorganized, elderly patient who is agitated but not intentionally violent, the family needs to develop a safe strategy to calm or restrain the patient. If no harm is imminent due to the patient's agitation, it may be most effective to keep a safe distance from the patient and speak calmly and soothingly. For example, "Dad, please try to calm down. You're safe at home. This is your son, John, and I'm going to stay right here with you. You are upset. Can we sit down and talk?" As the patient calms down, physical comforting, such as an arm around the shoulder or holding hands, can enhance the calming effect. If such verbal interventions are not productive, then the family must know the options they have to ensure everyone's safety. Direct physical restraint of the patient, for example, carrying the patient to his room or holding him down while he relaxes, should only be attempted if the family has sufficient numbers and strength to do this without harming the patient or themselves.

> A 70-year-old man developed Alzheimer's disease and at times became disoriented and agitated, throwing objects at home. His elderly wife would try to reason with him, but to no avail. He was clearly physically stronger than she was, and she was unable to restrain him. She had learned this the hard way the first time he became agitated, when she had attempted to get him to lie down. He struck her, breaking her nose. She had since worked out two options. During evenings and weekends, she could call her son, who lived nearby, to come and restrain her husband. The patient seemed to calm down quickly with his son present. When the son was unavailable, she could call the local police, who had been made aware of the situation by the son and had agreed to help.

Such interventions deal with the immediate problem, but planning should also address prevention of subsequent episodes. For the patient in this example, his episodes of agitation were greatly reduced after his wife made some additional efforts to keep him oriented (large calendar on the wall, signs identifying the various rooms in the house, leaving some lights on in the house at night) and after his physician placed him on a low dose of haloperidol.

Reducing aggression in someone with psychotic symptoms is a different matter. Consider the severely manic and grandiose patient who believes he is the focus of a worldwide plot (including his family) to assassinate him, or the occasional paranoid schizophrenic patient who is responding to hallucinations that command him to kill his neighbor. In both cases, the patient has a compelling, psychotic need to attack others. Such patients are in immediate need of treatment, particularly antipsychotic medication to reduce the psychotic symptoms. They usually require hospitalization as well. For a family to argue with such a patient about his delusions or hallucinations may only encourage aggression. These patients feel threatened by physical closeness. The family is ill-advised to attempt physical restraint. At best, they may be able to talk calmly to the patient from a safe distance, always maintaining a route of exit for themselves and the patient, while outside help (for example, police or mobile mental health team) is being summoned.

A more ambiguous and therefore more difficult situation for families is the risk of aggression in a patient with a psychotic disorder who has recompensated on medication, but who is in tenuous control under stress. For example, a 26-year-old woman suffered from recurrent manic psychoses that responded to antipsychotics and lithium carbonate, but she remained short-tempered even on the medications. When stressed she would break objects in the home. After various trials of medications to improve the patient's temperament, her psychiatrist advised the family that no further behavioral improvement could be achieved with medications. With the help of a family counselor, the family developed a set of clear expectations and limits for the patient. These included:

1) She would not damage property at home.

2. If she damaged property, she would pay for replacement of any property from her income earned as a part-time waitress.
3. If she failed at #1 and #2, she would have to find another place to live.

In general, behavioral contracts can be effective adjuncts to other therapies for controlling aggressive behavior. An example of a written behavioral contract was given in Chapter 6.

Patients with poor impulse control under stress can also benefit from various family activities to reduce stress. As described in the preceding chapter, these actions include reducing the unexpected, establishing clear routines and expectations for the patient, discussing and planning family decisions with the patient, allowing the patient to remove himself from stressful circumstances in the home (for example, visits by family friends), and communicating expectations clearly.

Although the aggressive behavior of demented, psychotic, or impulsive patients can cause much distress for families, the most troublesome type of aggression is the purposeful aggression toward family members by some patients. Typically these patients are diagnosed as suffering from some type of character disorder or recompensated psychotic disorder. They are not acting under any delusions, but behave in an abusive or openly hostile manner toward the family. The family feels intimidated by the patient and helpless to intervene because psychiatric treatment has either not reduced the behavior or actually inadvertently exacerbated it. For example, the patient may be angry with the family because they petitioned for his hospitalization.

A 30-year-old man diagnosed as having alcoholism and antisocial personality disorder had a history of multiple arrests for driving while intoxicated and multiple hospitalizations for detoxification. For his latest hospitalization, he was committed against his will at the request of his parents after he came home intoxicated and expressed suicidal ideation. After detoxifying, he expressed anger at his parents for committing him and alluded to "fixing" them. He lived near his parents and had dinner with them regularly once a week. The parents were doubtful that he would actually act against them, but were fearful because he had never before been so overtly hostile. They discussed this with the patient during family counseling sessions. It helped to air some old sources of contention between the patient and his parents. However, the parents and family counselor remained concerned about the patient's potential for aggression. Therefore, a behavioral contract was written. In it the patient agreed not to come to his parents' home intoxicated and not to make verbal or physical threats toward them. In return, he would continue to come for dinner once a week. If he violated the agreement, his parents would immediately call the local police, to whom he was well-known, and the police would remove him from their house. By agreeing to the police intervention beforehand, he accepted some responsibility for that decision, and the parents felt more comfortable actually calling for the police, if needed.

In our experience the family has only two acceptable options in such circumstances. The first is to develop a specific behavioral agreement that provides some reasonable assurance that the patient will refrain from aggression. This usually defuses the situation and permits ongoing contacts between patient and family. The second option is a legal one. For patients who repeatedly threaten their families, the family may need to obtain a legal order that restrains the patient from visiting them. This is obviously a distasteful choice, but is preferable to living in constant fear. The family clinician needs to make the family aware of this option and at times may need to encourage them to act on it.

We do not recommend reviewing in detail the possibility of violence and its management with all families, but we do feel that such efforts with selected families who are dealing with an aggressive relative is time well spent. Two principles must be reinforced with the families in dealing with violent patients. First, there is no reason for them to tolerate violence in the home. Second, the family need not feel that they have to contain all of the patient's violence; at times they can draw on outside sources of help, such as the police or a hospital. In discussions of these issues, the family may need to deal with their own feelings of guilt that they somehow have brought on or deserve the violent behavior or that they cannot expect the patient to be nonviolent because he is sick. Such feelings are common and ought to be explored with the family. As with many victims, families may respond by rationalizing the violence. They actually feel they somehow deserved it. This reaction is common and almost always unfounded, not withstanding the possibility that they may be able to alter their approach to the problem (as described above) to avert future violence by the patient.

CARELESSNESS

Careless behaviors by patients in the home can pose a safety hazard. These include such things as failing to turn off the stove, leaving candles or cigarettes burning in rooms, or leaving things lying on stairways or in the middle of the floor. Patients may be careless due to impaired judgment or reality-testing (as in schizophrenia), forgetfulness (as in Alzheimer's disease), neglect of self (as in depression), or lack of motivation (as in chronic schizophrenia). Families have a responsibility to ensure safety in the home. In addition, they can gradually place increasing responsibility on the patient to correct troublesome behaviors. Some families blindly assume full responsibility for picking up after the patient, resigning themselves to the misbelief that the patient cannot change. Other families become angry and reject the patient because of his or her carelessness.

To avoid these counterproductive responses, the family members can learn to identify what behaviors pose a safety threat. Then they can go on to identify why the patient might be doing those things. Here the therapist can be very useful. For example, the psychotic patient's perceptions of reality may be such that he is unable to use the stove and ought not to have access to matches. The family can identify these times of distorted reality perception and restrict the patient's behavior during them. On the other hand, the patient may simply not have the requisite skills to do certain things, such as operate a stove. In these situations, simple lessons, for example, how to use the stove, may be all that is needed. The family can provide this themselves, or the patient may attend a day program that focuses on these skills. Yet a third reason for carelessness can be the apathetic attitude of some schizophrenic patients, for example, not picking up after themselves. In such cases, the patient's behavior may be restricted and a set of conditions established to encourage the patient to be less careless. We will not repeat the procedure for behavioral contracting here, but these contracts can be very effective at controlling careless patient behaviors.

PSYCHOTIC SYMPTOMS AND BEHAVIORS

Psychosis takes a myriad of forms. Some symptoms respond to medication and pose no problem as long as the patient complies with treatment. Other symptoms may not respond, but really pose no problem, for example, minor rituals the patient performs in his room alone. Unfortunately, some psychotic symptoms persist or recur intermittently despite treatment and are troublesome to families. Here, also, the family can learn to identify them and decide with a clinician's help how to cope with them. For example, some patients express their delusions to family members in a persistent manner.

PATIENT: The mailman is the front man for the CIA extermination program. He looks OK, but he really isn't. Our mail has radioactive poisons in it. We shouldn't take the mail.

MOTHER: That's crazy talk, John. I'll have no more of it!

This scene recurred in this family on a daily basis and usually led to an argument between mother and son. She and her husband brought the problem to a family counseling session to solve. Using the problem-solving steps described in the preceeding chapter, they worked out the following:

Problem: John believes the mail is poisoned and argues with us about this.

Goal: John will gain better control of this persistent concern and the arguments will stop.

Alternatives:

1) Increase John's medication (previously tried, but not successful).
2) John will move to a group home (not acceptable to John or mother).
3) Arrangements will be made for mail to be delivered at next door neighbors, and mother will pick it up secretly (rejected because of inconvenience and because of concern that John would find out and implicate his neighbor and mother in his delusional ideas).
4) Behavioral contract to decrease the behavior (selected alternative).

Behavioral Contract:

1) John will not discuss his concerns about the mail.
2) For each morning that John does not mention these concerns, he will receive 5 points.
3) If John does mention his concerns, his mother will respond by saying, "John, I understand that you believe the mail is poisoned and that this frightens you. I don't believe the mail is poisoned, though, so try not to worry." If John persists, his mother will ignore the delusional comments and, if necessary, ask John to sit quietly in another room for 15 minutes (something that

had worked before but which the family did not regularly request of John).
4) Each weekend, John could spend his points on a variety of activities that he identified as enjoyable.

This behavioral contract worked. Although John remained
delusional about the mailman for some time, he did decrease
his preoccupation with the delusion and his annoying discussions with his mother.

What is hardest for families is understanding that no matter how unrealistic the delusion or hallucination, the patient
experiences it as reality. What is hardest for the patient to
deal with is at once accepting the subjective reality of the
symptom and learning that he need not respond to it. Arguing with the patient about it does not help. What can help is a
statement that the family member perceives things differently. For some patients, who are aware that some of their ideas
or perceptions are not real, it also helps for the family member
to differentiate between what is and is not real. For example,
in the case of John, the following dialogue would be helpful:

JOHN: The mail is poisoned.
MOTHER: John, I realize you believe the mail is poisoned and
       that this frightens you. I appreciate your concern for
       our safety. I don't believe the mail is poisoned, though.
JOHN: But I can smell something in the mail today.
MOTHER: Yes, one of the letters seems to smell like perfume.
       I smell that too, but that doesn't mean the mail is poi-
       soned. Remember how we discussed that sometimes you
       misinterpret things? I think this is one of those times.
       Why don't we relax and have a cup of coffee? We need
       to get together our grocery list.

This example also illustrates that while the patient may not
give up the psychotic symptom, his attention often can be
diverted to more realistic concerns, thus diminishing the importance of the symptom at the time as well as the problems
that arise interpersonally due to his preoccupation with it.

DRUG ABUSE

The use of street drugs and alcohol can exacerbate symptoms of psychosis, mania, and depression. One sign that suggests drug abuse is when the patient exhibits sudden erratic changes in behavior. For example, the patient may return from an evening out with friends and appear "out of it," confused, or unusually mellow or irritable. The family may find unidentified pills in the patient's room or smell marijuana smoke. The family members must be clear with the patient about their limits, expectations, and the consequences of drug use. Use of drugs while out with friends may require restriction of evening activites outside of the home. Abuse of drugs in the home may lead to other restrictions or even expulsion from the home. Practically speaking, it is usually difficult for the family to confirm that the patient is abusing drugs. They don't have easy access to lab tests. Therefore, we use an "index of suspicion" criterion. That is, if the family has strong reason to believe the patient is abusing drugs, they can proceed to initiate their contingencies without "absolute proof" that abuse has occurred.

A 19-year-old man with schizophrenia frequently smoked marijuana in the bathroom at home. The smell was obvious to his parents, but they never actually found any in his possession. He always claimed that he was smoking "tea, nothing illegal," and would declare that it was unfair of them to do anything because they had no proof. His parents felt frustrated because they didn't want to unjustly accuse him, yet remained convinced he was using marijuana. An uncomfortable stalemate existed.

In reviewing this situation, the family clinician pointed out that the parents were not functioning in a court of law and that they did not have to prove their case "beyond a reasonable shadow of doubt" in order to act. With this advice, they decided to institute a series of consequences whenever they suspected he had been smoking marijuana. These consequences included restriction of the patient to the house for three days and no visitors for the same time. They also made it clear to the patient that if he continued to use marijuana, he would have to live elsewhere. Unfortunately, in this case, the patient did continue to abuse drugs at home, restrictions only increased the friction between him and his parents, and his parents eventually insisted that he find his own apartment. He did so, but has been in and out of the hospital several times since for exacerbations of his psychosis related to PCP use.

Drug or alcohol abuse subverts treatment and poses a major obstacle to patient recovery when it occurs. The family and clinician can only do so much. The patient retains ultimate responsibility and when motivated can act to find other sources of gratification. The family helps first by identifying the problem and bringing it to the attention of the clinician. They also help by identifying this as a problem to the patient and establishing their rules and limits for him. The clinician evalutes the reasons for the patient's abuse of drugs. Is the patient trying to self-medicate unresolved symptoms of anxiety, depression, or psychosis? If so, a change in medication can relieve the drug abuse. Is the patient bored? If so, he may find relief in a day treatment program or sheltered workshop. Is he lonely and using drugs as a means to associate with peers? If this is the case, social skills training or a psychosocial club may help. In any event, progress can be impeded indefinitely by drug abuse and the problem requires high priority when it exists.

FINANCIAL IRRESPONSIBILITY

Even the most healthy among us sometimes find themselves in bankruptcy. There is no wonder that some patients have difficulty managing money. Their judgment is impaired, they are poor at reality-testing, or their financial schemes turn grandiose and doomed to fail. Our legal system holds families accountable for their relative's financial mismanagement. This poses a considerable problem when it occurs. The following examples show the range of problems that can arise.

A 23-year-old schizophrenic man received monthly Supplemental Security Income (SSI) checks. His mother, with whom he lived, was dependent on the checks to support the household. The patient would spend over half of this money each month at a local pool hall, his only source of social contact outside the home, where he would lose bets on games, buy others cigarettes, and occasionally lend money that was never repaid.

An 18-year-old manic-depressive woman, the daughter of a prominent, local chain store owner, had the habit of borrowing her parents' credit cards to buy large amounts of merchandise during manic episodes. Out of embarrassment they would pay these large bills rather than take action to stop her from using the credit cards.

A 70-year-old man who had achieved success as a businessman developed Alzheimer's disease. He began making errors in judgment due to confusion and signed away some valuable property for very little money before his family became aware of what was happening.

Whenever we encounter such situations in the course of working with a patient or family, we point out to the family members that they need not and ought not accept this financial burden. In some cases the solution may be relatively simple. For example, the patient may agree to turn his SSI check over to the family so that they can help him manage it. A regular allowance can be given the patient on a weekly basis. This is particularly useful in helping a patient learn to manage his money. If he spends it all in one place, he has nothing left for the rest of the week. There is an incentive to budget.

In other cases, the solution may be more complex and require legal advice. We are cautious not to give legal advice, but we do advise families to seek it when it seems necessary, such as when they are facing unnecessary and significant financial risk due to their relative's irresponsible behavior. Legal options vary from state to state according to the circumstances. In the first case above, the mother was able to have herself named as a co-payee, so that the SSI checks were deposited directly into a bank account and funds could be withdrawn only if both she and her son signed. The family in the second case had their daughter declared emancipated from them, so that they were not responsible for her bills. They stopped lending her their credit cards and took legal action to relieve themselves of responsibility when she used the cards without their consent. These actions meant that the daughter could be charged with credit card theft by the credit company. This potential consequence turned out to be a major deterrent to future abuse by her. The man in the third case was declared legally incompetent to manage his finances, and his wife was named his conservator.

NONCOMPLIANCE WITH TREATMENT

The family is often expected to assume responsibility for monitoring the patient's compliance with medication, making sure the patient keeps appointments and attends programs, and coordinating visits with residential care programs. Each of these areas deserves some specific discussion. With regard to medication, it is important that families understand what type and dosage schedule of medication the patient receives, the rationale for the medication (including the importance of taking the medicine everyday), and the expected and realistic results of the medication. The goal is for them to develop a supportive attitude about the medication. The clinician can facilitate the family members' role in this regard by first taking the time to explain the medication to them and then providing them with reading materials on the type of medication prescribed, including information on indications for the medicine and its side effects. Time should be taken to answer their questions and hear their concerns.

This discussion with the family also helps to clarify the family members' attitudes toward medication and identifies any problems they may have in supporting the treatment. For example, a schizophrenic woman in the hospital responded well to antipsychotics but expressed very negative attitudes about the medication. She could not specify what she did not like about the medicine and objectively she did not appear to be experiencing any side effects. She would return to the hospital from weekend passes home in a more decompensated state. Over time her attitude became more positive toward the medication, but she continued to fail to comply whenever she went on a home visit. This pattern constituted a major impediment to her discharge. After puzzling about this situation, the staff finally interviewed her grandmother, who was her main support, and found that the grandmother was very negative about any type of medication. The patient's mother was also diagnosed as schizophrenic and had not done well on medication. This experience had contributed significantly to the grandmother's dim view of medicine. Unfortunately, repeated discussions with the grandmother failed to sway her views, and the patient remained in the hospital because of continued relapses.

Concerns about the patient's compliance with treatment often focus on medication, but compliance with other aspects of treatment can be just as important. As we now know, psychosocial interventions, such as continuing day treatment programs, prevocational and vocational workshop activities, psychosocial clubs, behavioral contracts and a variety of other treatment programs, can be crucial in the rehabilitation of the discharged mental patient (Caton, 1984; Bellack, 1984). Only by taking an active and willing role can the patient benefit from these types of programs. It is in regard to these modalities of treatment that the patient's social withdrawal and passivity may take the heaviest toll. It is one thing to get the patient to swallow pills at home; it is quite another to get the patient to spend four hours during the day at a program that demands his active participation. Families who successfully persist in getting the patient to take medication often throw up their arms in despair with regard to getting the patient to do much more. We cannot underestimate the importance of reinforcing family members' understanding of the role that psychosocial treatments play in recovery from mental illness. Without the family's active support, there is often little chance that a passive, withdrawn patient will attend programs outside of the home. Even with this active support, some patients remain noncompliant and resistant to all suggestions by family and clinician alike. Being supportive of the family members' efforts in these situations will encourage them to be patient with their troubled relative.

Setting a realistic timetable may help. A five-year plan that succeeds beats five one-year plans that do not. For a chronic schizophrenic patient, the goal for the entire first year after discharge may be to achieve the patient's compliance with medications and to remain out of the hospital. During the subsequent year the patient may begin to attend a day treatment program or psychosocial club. The third year may see the patient progress to a group home setting or sheltered workshop. The next two years may be devoted simply to keeping the patient at this level of function. Helping the family and patient adjust their expectations to this modest, long-term time frame can be a major step toward improving patient and family satisfaction with his progress. It also eliminates the discouragement felt after the failure of an overly optimistic short-term plan.

Attending an outpatient treatment program requires various behavioral steps on the part of the patient. He has to get up on time, organize himself and be ready to leave for the program when necessary. He must be able to get to the program, which may require use of public transportation. He will have to tolerate at least brief group activities and social contacts. After participating in the program, he has to get home, a task easy for us, but not for a troubled individual. Finally, the toll exacted by traveling to and from the program and participating in it must not be so high that he is more dysfunctional at home. These are no small tasks for the recovering patient, and families may need help in recognizing the complexity of the task as well as the stepwise approach they can take in helping the patient attend programs.

Along with being tolerant and supportive at home, family members often can act as the patient's advocate with regard to the treatment system. First, they have to be aware of the various types of programs available so that they can work with the patient and the therapist in selecting the most appropriate one. The patient may be inappropriately placed in a sheltered workshop that requires a minimum of 15 hours per week attendance when he can only handle five hours per week. Unfortunately, many treatment programs are unwilling to tolerate sporadic patient attendance and frequently discontinue the patient's enrollment when the patient does not live up to their expectations. The family may bear the burden of seeing that the right type of program is selected. Secondly, the family may need to lobby strongly with the treatment program so that the patient who attends sporadically is not shut out. Some programs are more willing to tolerate patient noncompliance when they know the family is making every effort to see that the patient does attend. Conversely, programs may more readily terminate the patient when they perceive that not only is the patient noncompliant, but so is the family.

Families often play an important role in maintaining the patient away from home in a residential treatment program. Deciding that a patient should move out of the family home into a group home setting is not easy, and patients and families both may experience second thoughts. They look at a group home arrangement with other disturbed persons and fear that somehow they are relinquishing their responsibilities to their child and abandoning him to a setting that, at least by their perception, may not be much different from the hospital. In our experience the two most common issues in connection with residential care are: 1) initial resistance to having the patient live in a group home setting; and 2) difficulties in supporting the patient to stay in the group home. The counselor should try to explain the positive aspects of the group home service and encourage families and the patient to look at different homes before one is selected. Homes differ dramatically in the amount of programming they provide and in the quality of their environments. Trying to find the right fit between the patient and a group home can prove difficult. The patient and family often face very limited options due to the shortage of such homes. Once a patient has entered a residential program, he may be ambivalent about staying there and prefer to come back to the family home. The family members may want the patient to stay in the group home, but they feel guilty about telling the patient that he has to sleep at the group home and take his meals there. To sustain contact with their families, patients sometimes spend weekends or one night a week at home. Such limited contact supports the patient's increasing independence from the family and integration into a group home while satisfying the patient's and family's needs for ongoing contact.

PANHANDLING

Lack of gainful employment is a serious problem for many of the chronically mentally ill, and some deal with their lack of money by panhandling. Such behavior can be extremely embarrassing and upsetting to families, particularly when the patient does this with neighbors and friends. Sometimes the family doesn't know this is happening because it occurs in distant locations. But when it does occur near their home, they can intervene.

A 19-year-old schizophrenic patient became angry when his parents refused to buy him a new radio unless he completed certain daily chores at home. He resorted to standing on the corner of their block, asking for money. After their son asked several neighbors for money, the embarrassed parents decided on the following plan.

1) They asked their neighbors not to give their son money and to contact them whenever he asked them for some.
2) They contacted the local police, who agreed to monitor his panhandling behavior in the course of their usual neighborhood rounds and to bring him home (or charge him with panhandling) when caught.
3) With these restrictions and monitoring mechanisms in place, they developed a behavioral contract with the patient with points gained for performing the household chores and points lost for episodes of panhandling. With sufficient points the patient would be able to buy his new radio.

The 30-year-old daughter of a prominent and well-liked couple had the habit of calling her parents' friends to ask for money. These friends typically took pity on the patient (and by implication on her parents) and gave her money. Her parents were mortified when they discovered that this was happening. After two highly emotional sessions with the family clinician, which focused on their shame, anger, and guilt, they were able to ask their friends to stop acquiescing to their daughter's requests and to inform them when such requests occurred. They discussed the problem with their daughter and developed a behavioral strategy similar to that in the case above to help their daughter earn money at home.

INAPPROPRIATE SEXUAL BEHAVIORS

Patients sometimes engage in sexual behaviors that cause distress for family and others and that may jeopardize the patient's well-being or safety. Issues of sexuality are difficult enough in the lives of most people, but when an adult patient behaves in sexually inappropriate ways, the effects can be at best embarrassing and at worst tragic for patient and family.

The manic-depressive 19-year-old daughter of a first-generation Chinese immigrant family became sexually preoccupied and active during her manic episodes. At such times she would engage in sexual acts with several men in the local college dormitory and would usually be arrested for public nudity. Such behavior was deeply shocking to her parents and a source of great shame for them. She would also make sexually lewd comments to her father and, of most concern to her family, to her revered grandfather.

A 30-year-old woman with chronic schizophrenia had very low self-esteem, was quite passive, and could be easily persuaded by men to engage in sexual acts. To her family's dismay and horror, she would go with men whom she did not know and engage in sex (sometimes for money). On more than one occasion, she returned home beaten and disheveled. The patient was not psychotic at these times, expressed a distaste for sex, but seemed to lack the ability to say "no" to men.

A 20-year-old man with schizophrenia became increasingly psychotic at home. He began masturbating in front of his 12-year-old sister and would laugh inappropriately when told to stop.

Each of these cases illustrates the need for various approaches to helping the family cope with inappropriate sexual behaviors. In the case of the 19-year-old manic woman, the major clinical intervention was lithium carbonate maintenance therapy. Unfortunately, she was only intermittently compliant. The family clinician discussed with the parents the pattern of hypersexuality associated with mania. Although this helped them to understand the patient's behavior in terms of her illness and the importance of medication compliance, it did little to quell their sense of shame. The family clinician encouraged them to discuss their feelings in the context of their Chinese culture. They agreed to a strategy to at least reduce the embarrassment within the family. First, the patient was not allowed into their home when she showed signs of hypomania (or mania) or when she was not taking her lithium. Second, she was not permitted to use the family's phone to talk to their relatives in China within two weeks of an episode of inappropriate sexual behavior or lewd remarks. These restrictions were sufficient to increase the patient's compliance somewhat and decreased her opportunities to cause embarrassment for her parents in relation to their extended family.

For the second woman with chronic schizophrenia the main problem was passivity due to schizophrenic negative symptoms, poor self-esteem due to her chronic disability, and poor social judgment. Her family developed a more structured schedule for her time at home, which decreased her excursions out to local hangouts. They also consulted a local day treatment program, and the patient was enrolled in assertiveness training. With time she became more assertive and the incidents of sexual abuse decreased. In talking to this woman, it also became apparent that she had only a vague understanding of human sexuality and in particular of the mechanisms of pregnancy and birth control. Her parents indicated that they had never felt comfortable discussing these things with her. Therefore, she also enrolled in a sex education class at the day program.

In the situation of the psychotic young man who masturbated at home, a series of steps helped the family to cope with the situation. First, they were advised by the family clinician that this behavior was part of the patient's psychosis (he believed he expelled demons by masturbating). Second, their instinct to protect their daughter from exposure to this behavior was reinforced. The patient was escorted to his room by his father at the first sign that the behavior was about to occur. Third, they contacted the patient's psychiatrist, who increased his medications. Fourth, the patient was told clearly that he could not behave this way, except in his own room.

Working with families to help them cope with such sexual behaviors requires an open attitude and comfort on the part of the clinician. The forbidden nature of the topic must be dispelled so that the family can discuss the problem constructively, and the clinician must be sensitive to the family's cultural, religious, and personal values with regard to sexuality. As with the other problem behaviors discussed, family members need to understand that they do not have to tolerate inappropriate sexual behaviors at home and that they may need to consult with the clinician or other supports (for example, police) at times to deal with these.

INSTITUTIONALIZED BEHAVIORS

Deinstitutionalization has decreased the risks of institutionalism in many patients, but unfortunately patients at times still acquire a variety of habits and behaviors in institutions that detract from their ability to cope outside. These behaviors are usually relatively benign, for example, eating all food with a spoon or fingers, gulping food, rocking movements, and passivity. To some extent these behaviors are related to diagnosis, particularly chronic schizophrenia, but the environment can play a major role. These behaviors can often be decreased by consistent interventions and raised expectations in the home. For example, the parents may need to remind the patient to use his fork and knife as well as his spoon, or to eat more slowly. Behavioral contracts can be used if simple reminders are ineffective. The family may want to arrange trips out of the house (or hospital) in order to help the patient reacclimate to the non-institutional world. Sometimes a friend of the patient, volunteer companion, or case manager can be very helpful in this regard.

In this chapter we have explained approaches for helping families to cope with a variety of problem behaviors commonly encountered in the mentally ill at home: social withdrawal and passivity, suicidality, aggression, carelessness, psychotic symptoms, drug abuse, financial irresponsibility, noncompliance with treatment, panhandling, inappropriate sexual behavior, and institutionalized behaviors. The approaches build on the family's basic skills as a problem-solving unit. Problem behaviors need to be identified and, to the degree possible, understood in the context of the patient's illness and psychological state. The family then systematically plans how to deal with the situation, remaining cognizant of two important principles. First, they need not and ought not make dramatic alterations in their lives to accommodate the patient's problem behaviors. Second, they need to know when they require outside help (for example, police or hospital) and how to go about getting it.

8

HELPING FAMILY MEMBERS
HELP THEMSELVES

Up to this point we have focused on helping the family to help the patient. However, each family member faces emotional issues regarding the illness in the family's midst, individual decisions about his or her own life, and conflicts with other family members about how day-to-day problems should be handled. In addition, each person faces the problem of stigma and isolation that mental illness in the family inevitably brings. In this chapter, we discuss each of these issues with advice on how the mental health worker can help family members find a balance between addressing their own needs and meeting those of the ill member.

CHRONICITY AND MOURNING

One of the most difficult tasks facing each family member is coming to grips with the chronicity of the illness. This involves grieving lost expectations, developing a more realistic view of what the ill family member will be able to accomplish given the deficits and vulnerabilities that remain, and finding a compromise between martyring oneself in the service of the ill person and behaving callously or irresponsibly. Inevitably, each family member will approach this task in his or her own way, with each reaching different decisions. It is the counselor's task to facilitate this process, helping family members negotiate the differences of opinion which are certain to arise.

In doing so, the counselor must face the fact that there are no "right" answers, and that what is right for one family member may be wrong for another.

The mourning process involves accepting that certain symptoms or aspects of the illness may be more or less permanent. For example, the mental impairment may limit the patient's ability to hold a job commensurate with socioeconomic status and education, to live independently, or to marry and raise a family. A mental health professional with a schizophrenic sibling put it this way:

> As the reality of the situation begins to sink in, you begin to realize that the person you had seen growing up, in whom you had hope, for whom you had expectations for a good life, is not going to make it; the potential that you had seen is not going to be tapped. Talents, such as woodworking or athletics, are overwhelmed by the mental disorder. Instead of growing up, maturing, and realizing everyone's expectations, the ill relative seems to fall apart as others his age pass him by.
> . . . You sit in the car together, you go places and do things together, but all the while it is not the relative you once knew. The conflict between physical life and dead hopes is constantly there. (Bernheim, Lewine, and Beale, 1982, p. 32)

For many family members (including the ill person), accepting the chronicity of the illness (at least in terms of functional deficits) occurs gradually, after repeated crises or a very lengthy hospitalization. For others, insight waxes and wanes, with periods of acceptance interspersed with periods of renewed grief and frustration. As one mother put it:

> Each time there was that great white hope—maybe this time she'll stay on a fairly even keel, you can live with it. (Bernheim, Lewine and Beale, 1982, p. 36)

As a clinician you can help family members through this process in several ways. First, encourage them to talk about what their expectations had been, evaluating each with respect to what the ill person seems capable of achieving. In many instances, goals can be modified rather than given up completely. For example, a person might not be able to marry, but may be able, through psychosocial clubs and social skills training, to develop a supportive, nurturing peer group, thus avoiding the utter loneliness the family might have feared.

Second, help the family acknowledge and take pleasure in gains that are made – in successful transition to a halfway house, in an evening out together without incident, in the ill person's learning to use public transportation alone. Focusing on short-term goals that are in line with the ill member's capacities can reduce disappointment. As one mother put it:

> I don't hope for the things I hoped for before. I just hope that Steve can take care of his own personal needs, that alone. This way I'm not as disappointed, and if he does make progress, at least . . . that's extra. (Bernheim, Lewine, and Beale, 1982, p. 43)

Third, prepare the family for the possibility of relapse. Families who expect ups and downs are less likely to become unduly frustrated when symptoms reemerge. They can learn to hope for shorter hospitalizations with longer periods of adequate functioning in the community rather than no hospitalizations at all.

Hospitalization need not be seen by professionals as a failure. If they do equate hospitalization with failure, then the patient and family will do so as well. Too often, societal and bureaucratic pressures produce an anti-hospital bias in the therapist so that readmission is seen as always preventable and to be avoided. However, hospitalization is more reasonably viewed as an intervention in the service of reducing the length or severity of a psychotic episode, an intervention that provides both protection for a patient who may need it and respite for the family. It may prove necessary from time to time despite the best efforts of the ill person, the family, and the treatment team. In fact, avoiding hospitalization in a futile effort to keep a worsening patient in the community may have seriously deleterious effects. This situation probably occurs far more often than it should. Destigmatizing hospitalization can reduce the patient's and family's guilt and resistance in the event that the illness makes inpatient treatment necessary.

Finally, the long-term prognosis for many of the chronically mentally ill may not be as pessimistic as was once believed. Acute symptoms tend to become less florid and troublesome over the years and many people attain a surprisingly high level of functioning within the community at 20- to 30-year follow-up (Harding, Zubin, and Strauss, in press). The counselor can make family members aware of these data so that they can look forward to a time when their burden will be, if not gone, at least lightened.

A LIFE OF ONE'S OWN

Each family member faces innumerable decisions about how to live in the face of the long-term caretaking responsibilities for the mentally ill relative. As in families with aged parents at home or those with physically disabled children, the issue of which sacrifices to make and which to avoid is ever present.

Rarely does living one's life in the service of the ill member represent a satisfactory (or satisfying) adjustment. Rather, people who take this route are at risk for depleting their own emotional resources and paradoxically placing a heavy burden on the ill person, who then becomes responsible for the emotional well-being of his parent, spouse, child, or sibling. More effective solutions are found by family members who limit their sacrifices, develop personal goals and activities outside of caretaking, and in general pay attention to their own needs.

In this area conflicts among family members can be expected. Parents of an ill young adult cannot understand why the well siblings don't show more interest in their brother or sister, why they aren't more "understanding." A wife resents her husband's working late hours and leaving her alone with his ill mother. A husband pressures his wife to take a vacation with him, but she protests that she feels guilty about leaving their ill child alone. In addition to helping each person in the family find some personal satisfaction and sustenance, the counselor is involved in helping the family members understand and accept each other's needs and negotiate mutually agreeable solutions.

We begin by inquiring how much time each family member spends on hobbies, athletics, or other leisure activities. Often we find that at least one family member (typically the mother, if the ill person is an adolescent or young adult) has virtually no relief from caretaking responsibilities. In fact, we often have to go back a number of years to help the person recall how he or she used to spend time before the relative became ill. We then ask the family to work together to encourage and make it possible for the person to reinvest some time and energy in one or more of these areas, which may include reading, sports, crafts, volunteer work, gardening, employment, political involvement, or a host of other activities. We try to develop a concrete plan which specifies the activity, the specific times which will be allotted to it, and what other family members will do to ensure that the time is made available. We counter resistance by pointing out that each person's "batteries" need to be "recharged" if he or she is to be able to continue providing for loved ones. That is, we reframe "selfishness" as "selflessness."

As this work proceeds, it is possible that the family's equilibrium as a system will become somewhat disturbed. If the mother, for example, begins to take more time for her own activities, it may leave the father or a sibling with more caretaking responsibility. These issues should be anticipated in advance, if at all possible, and discussed openly, in order to avoid making plans which the family cannot or will not keep. In keeping with our general style, we tentatively suggest changes rather than dictating them, always keeping in mind that the family's struggle to provide for each member's needs is a difficult one at best. We respect their intuition when they tell us that a particular plan can't work, since they know each other far better than we know any of them. We aim for small changes that allow family members to retain their own individual styles of coping and adaptation.

Not only do we try to develop such a plan for each family member who seems to need it, but we also work in a similar way with the parental couple. Often, parents of the mentally ill person become so caught up in caretaking concerns that their interactions involve little else. We try to get them to set aside certain times of day when they will talk about their child's problems, its effects on the family and related decisions, and to refrain from such discussions at other times, enjoying each other and mutual activities. Again, they may have to engage in some recollecting and fantasizing to come up with satisfying ways to spend time together, as well as some problem-solving to figure out how they can make this time available on the regular basis.

Once family members have become convinced of the value of non-caretaking goals and activities, they will need to explore creative ways to give themselves some respite from constant attention to the needs of the ill child, spouse, or parent. For example, families who have joined a support group may be able to trade caretaking services, leaving their ill member with another family for a weekend in return for taking the other family's ill member during a later weekend. They may discover that, given information and support, certain members of the extended family would be willing and able to look after the ill person for several hours or even several days. Some families have hired a college student as a "friend" for an ill young adult, thereby providing some respite on a regular basis. In Rochester, New York, this sort of arrangement has been formalized (without fee) by an organization called "compeer," which carefully matches community volunteers and patients (of all ages), providing psychiatric support by

the patient's physician to the visiting friend. Partial hospitalization, day programs, psychosocial clubs and community
residences may also be explored at this point. Some families,
of course, find that their ill relative is more capable of providing for himself or herself than they had imagined possible, once they are willing to risk finding out.

For some families, compassion and permission from the
mental health professional are enough to provoke more adaptive patterns of living. For others, mired in guilt and long-
standing denial of personal needs in the service of the ill
member, a series of concrete short-term behavioral goals can
help family members become more fulfilled and autonomous.

> A woman whose concern about the safety and well-
> being of her 27-year-old schizophrenic son prevented
> her from leaving her house agreed, after much coax-
> ing, to begin to do so in small steps. First, she left him
> only long enough to walk to the end of the block and
> back, no more than seven minutes. After two weeks
> she was able to stop and visit with a neighbor for a
> few minutes before returning home. Gradually, as her
> anxiety decreased, she began to enjoy these walks,
> and to trust her son's ability to manage on his own
> for brief periods of time. Several months later, she
> was shopping for groceries and clothes and visiting
> with other family members. She was able to leave her
> son alone for three to four hours without substantial
> discomfort.

FAMILY CONFLICTS

Sometimes one family member's style of dealing with
stress is to invest deeply in activities outside the family. It
is fairly typical, for example, to find that well siblings of
young schizophrenics become so active with school, sports,
or friends that they are rarely at home. Later, they go off to
college or work, often moving several hundred miles away
and visiting infrequently. They voice deep ambivalence about

the prospect of becoming responsible for their ill sibling when their parents die. Inevitably, their parents feel neglected and angry, although the pattern may be adaptive from the young person's perspective. (Parenthetically, these siblings often wind up in human service careers where they can put their frustrated need to be of help to good use.)

While this problem, as well as others like it, is not immediately resolvable, it sometimes helps to have family members share their feelings and the reasons for their decisions with each other, in the presence of a counselor who models respect for individual differences and acknowledges the grief that the illness has caused everybody by interfering with normal family life. Parents can be helped to understand that it is the siblings' love and intensely painful wish for things to be different that make visits infrequent, rather than purposeful neglect or callousness. Siblings can learn to recognize that their parents' "guilt trips" reflect the same frustrated wish that the family could function as if the illness did not exist. In this way, while much sadness remains, some of the anger and sense of estrangement can be relieved.

Another area of conflict which arises frequently involves differences of opinion about how the ill member should be treated. Should he be asked to do household chores or is getting him to follow through on these requests more trouble than it is worth? Should he live at home despite the detrimental effects his presence has on other family members, when good alternatives are unavailable? Should he be taken to family gatherings despite his embarrassing behavior or left at home? And, who should make these decisions, anyway?

It is natural for parents to have differences of opinion about how a child should be raised. When that child has a chronic mental illness, those differences are magnified since the consequences of "wrong" decisions can appear devastating. Further, when a child has a chronically incapacitating illness, there is no relief in the present or future from the responsibility of making caretaking decisions. In addition, as the siblings reach adulthood, they may or may not want input into the process, thus complicating the problem.

In helping the family resolve these difficulties, we keep several ideas in the forefront. First, there are no clear-cut "right" and "wrong" answers. What works best for one patient in one family may work poorly for another patient in another family. We try to translate "Should we . . . ?" into "Might it work best for us if we . . . ?"

Second, the consequences of choosing a less satisfactory (in hindsight) alternative are rarely as catastrophic as family members might have envisioned. We help them learn to ask themselves, "What is the worst that can happen if we decide this issue in this way?"

Third, we point out that strategies that fail offer as much useful information as strategies that succeed. After airing differences of opinion, we try to get the family members to *tentatively* adopt a particular decision, carry it out consistently, and evaluate the outcome clearly. We ask them to act like researchers, who admit they don't know the answer to a question and go about testing their hunches by devising experiments that produce data.

Finally, we help the family members articulate the decision-making process and chain of command that works best for them. For some families, an open democratic process (one person=one vote) works best. For others, the parents need to reach a consensus. For perhaps the majority, one member, the primary caretaker, solicits opinions and information but retains the right to make the final decision. We try to help families explore what patterns have worked best for them in the past and develop clarity about how best to handle future decisions.

Often a decision affects some family members but not others. For example, a sibling has to decide whether to visit the ill person in the hospital. Or a mother must decide whether to insist on chores when she will have to enforce any decision which is made. Others may have an opinion, but the final decision rests with the person affected. In these cases, we try to help the family decide "who owns the problem" by specifying the person or persons for whom consequences will occur when a decision is made.

We see these conflicts within the family as normal and inevitable, rather than as a result of family system pathology. The balance between meeting one's own needs and those of loved ones is precarious in normal circumstances. Its attainment is complicated immeasurably by the presence of mental illness in the family. Stylistic differences, communication problems, and emotional distress, which exist to some extent in all families, are exacerbated by any chronic illness or stress. These difficulties do not reflect personal or system failures; rather, they reflect normal problems in living that must be negotiated as best one can, with faith that others in the family are also doing the best they can.

COPING WITH STIGMA AND ISOLATION

Families report that chronic mental illness in a family member has an isolating effect on the family as a whole, as well as on each member individually. This occurs gradually through a combination of factors.

First, most people believe that mental illness reflects some deficiency in how a person was treated as a child. This is particularly true when symptoms emerge in adolescence or young adulthood, as is true of schizophrenia and many cases of bipolar illness, as well as most of the character disorders. Extended family and friends often communicate in subtle or not so subtle ways that the parents are at fault. Parents themselves are predisposed to accept this burden of guilt. Rather than face real or imagined accusations, they may choose to withdraw from contact. While this factor has an impact most directly on the parents, it also affects the siblings, who may feel both protective of and angry with their parents. They too may withdraw from interactions which stimulate these conflicted feelings.

In addition, the family faces the embarrassment engendered by the patient's behavior. Talking to voices, conversational non sequiturs, poor grooming, pacing, and accusations against the family are examples of behaviors that the family finds difficult to explain and that upset and frighten guests.

Rather than confront these behaviors, extended family and friends may stay away. Rather than cause discomfort, families may choose not to socialize with the patient present. If there are difficulties in finding someone to watch the patient or if the parents feel guilty leaving the patient, they may find that they have few opportunities for socializing without the patient.

Friends may also withdraw because they don't know if the family members want to talk about the problem. They don't want to appear nosy or prying; they don't want to embarrass, insult, or offend family members. The illness is treated in the same way that alcoholism is often treated – everyone knows but nobody talks about it.

In sum, families often feel that holding on to an active social support system is more trouble than it is worth. However, in the absence of extrafamilial supports, caring for the ill member can become the draining, frustrating focus of life.

One of the first steps the counselor can take to reduce isolation of family members is to put them in touch with others who have similar problems. Groups for families, either professionally led or grass roots, may come to replace the indigenous support system that has been given up. Attending a meeting of one of these groups, one is impressed by the atmosphere of warmth, support and respect – in short, of "family." For other families, the group is also a springboard to greater openness at home, since the group process not only lessens guilt and shame but also provides role models for self-disclosure.

Families who have successfully "come out of the closet" generally report a reduction of stress. Energy they once used to hide, excuse, or ignore the illness is made available for more constructive purposes. They are often surprised and delighted to find that others are capable of a great deal more understanding and support than they had expected.

> One mother reported that after years of keeping
> the illness in the family a secret, she finally told her
> boss about her daughter's condition. No longer did

she have to make excuses for leaving work briefly in the middle of the day to check on the situation at home. Not only did her employer tolerate these interruptions, but he also began to ask about how things were going and to express interest in learning about the illness. After this experience, she began to invite friends to the home, warning them in advance that her daughter was mentally ill and might not come out of her room or might wander through without greeting anyone. She emphasized that her daughter was not dangerous, only odd. She encouraged her friends to ask her any questions they might have and to voice both their curiosity and their concerns. Again, she was surprised to find that most people became quite comfortable at her home after a few visits and, better yet, that she was comfortable having them there. As a result, her daughter experienced a more nearly normal family life and she and her husband experienced some relief from caretaking duties.

In addition to providing support for the family, educating others about the illness can also reduce unreasonable demands and hostility directed at the patient. A grandparent, for example, who is taught about negative symptoms may learn not to ask, "Why can't a big strong boy like you do more work around the house for your parents?" Families have little to lose and much to gain in combatting myths and misconceptions. After all, others usually know that something is dreadfully wrong in the family. They are usually misinformed, by gossip and by their own preconceptions, about the true nature of the problem, its cause, how they can be of help, and how the family would like them to behave.

Helping families reduce their isolation involves working with them on developing answers to two questions: 1) "Whom should I tell?" and 2) "What should I tell?" It is useful to suggest that families "go public" gradually, choosing first someone whom they feel is likely to be sympathetic or whose support would be valuable to the family. If anyone in the family is hesitant to tell a particular person, it is probably best to wait. In other words, the family members should agree, if possible, on the person to be told first, so that disclosure will be both successful and rewarding. Depending upon the family system, one member may assume the role of liaison with extended family and friends, as was true in the case discussed above, or various family members may link up with their own friends.

How is the family to proceed if the ill person adamantly opposes any public discussion of the problem? While the family can certainly be encouraged to discuss this issue further and attempt to negotiate an agreement about whom to tell what, family members should understand that they are not bound by the patient's wishes – just as he or she is not bound by theirs. They can certainly share with selected family and friends that their relative's odd behaviors are the result of an illness for which he or she is being treated. They can tell the truth about why they must forgo a party or a trip out of town. They can voice their fears and frustrations. For relatives or friends who will be in contact with the ill person, information may be critical to their ability to maintain a calm, supportive posture and to handle psychotic behaviors in a helpful way. The immediate family must be able to share what it has learned in order to provide the widest possible support system for the ill member.

The "what" of telling depends partially upon the "whom" of telling. Information that is brief, concise, and doesn't overload the recipient with more than he or she wants to know is best. For example, it may be enough for the patient's teenage sister to tell her friends:

> My brother has mental problems. He acts sort of spacey, like sometimes he talks to these voices he hears in his head. He's not dangerous or anything. I wanted you to know about him before you came over so it wouldn't scare you or make you feel real uncomfortable. You can say "hi" and all to him, but don't be surprised if he doesn't answer you.

If a sibling chooses not to invite friends over due to the ill person's behavior, he or she might decide to say:

> Listen, I don't have people over to my house very often because my brother has a mental illness and he's sort of unpredictable and makes people uncomfortable. I didn't want you to think I was snobby or didn't like you or anything.

A complaining, intrusive grandparent might have to be told:

> Sue's doctor told us it was part of her illness to sleep a lot and stay by herself a lot for the first several months after she got out of the hospital. We know you might feel differently, but we think it's best not to push her to be more active just yet.

The counselor can help each family member identify people he or she would like to communicate with about the illness by working through the pros and cons of self-disclosure, being careful to point out any unrealistically negative consequences the person might fear. We find it helpful to suggest that people ask themselves, "What is the worst that might happen if I tell this person something about our situation?" Then, with the counselor they can decide what aspects of the problem they can reveal with a sense of safety and comfort. Role-playing can be valuable in helping family members anticipate unexpected responses and in rehearsing various ways of saying what needs to be said. Most people find initial disclosure the most difficult, with extended practice (and ongoing education so that they have a vocabulary to use and the self-confidence to use it) lightening the task as time goes on.

We find it useful to anticipate with families that the initial response to self-disclosure might be shock or subtle withdrawal (similar, no doubt, to some of their own first feelings), but this does not mean that the recipient of the information will not become knowledgeable and supportive in the long run. If family members can adopt a matter-of-fact attitude and persevere in communicating, stigma generally fades gradually.

Mental illness in the family disrupts each member's plans for the future. It disrupts family relationships by highlighting natural disagreements, differences in coping styles, and communication problems. It disrupts the family's relationship with the larger social support network as the stigma of mental illness provokes a conspiracy of silence. Goal-setting, supportive counseling, and behavioral rehearsal are all strategies that the counselor can enlist to help ameliorate these problems, so that each family member can live as normal and as fulfilling a life as possible under the circumstances.

9

THE FAMILY
AS ADVOCATE

Chronic mental illness brings the family into reluctant contact with the complex, unwieldy, often frustrating bureaucracy that has been characterized as the "mental health maze." It rarely happens that a chronically mentally ill person stays involved with a single treatment team over the course of the illness. Rather, various combinations of inpatient facilities, outpatient facilities, residential facilities, and rehabilitation programs will be involved at different times. Diagnostic uncertainty, medication changes and conflicting advice are the rule rather than the exception. It takes a formidable combination of knowledge, perseverance, and assertiveness to negotiate this maze successfully. Further, since the ill person is often not in a position to make considered decisions about treatment options, the family is faced with advocating for what the patient needs in the face of his apathy or even active resistance. The professional who takes the time to teach family members how to seek the best help available from among the many mental health agencies provides an invaluable service.

DEVELOPING EXPERTISE

Providing education about the illness is, of course, the first step. While we have discussed this issue in some detail in Chapter 5, several points bear additional discussion in the present context. The family needs to learn to evaluate the adequacy and certainty of the diagnosis in order to make informed choices about treatment. The following questions should be addressed as early in the educational program as possible:

1) How are psychiatric diagnoses arrived at? What are the roles of the family history, personal history, current symptomatology, and laboratory tests in making a diagnosis?
2) How certain is the diagnosis in this particular case?
3) What alternative diagnoses might be entertained? What steps can be taken to develop an adequate differential diagnosis?

Through suggested readings, group educational seminars, and individual consultation, the family (and often the patient as well) can be brought to a realistic appraisal of what is and is not understood about this particular illness.

Far too often we hear a parent report: "They said my son was schizophrenic, but now they think he is manic-depressive. What does that mean? Can he be both? Has he changed from one to the other? What do we do now?"

We like to use the phrase "working diagnosis" when communicating with families in order to emphasize our orderly, hypothesis-testing approach to diagnosis and treatment. We make families aware that diagnosis is often clarified through evaluating the patient's response to various treatments.

Once the diagnostic question has been addressed, treatment issues can be considered in the same fashion:

1) How and why is a particular medication at a particular dosage prescribed? How does one evaluate its efficacy? What alternatives will be pursued given various outcomes?
2) What are the data concerning the effectiveness of dietary interventions, orthomolecular treatments and other treatments about which the family has heard or read?

3) What are the roles of ancillary treatments including psychosocial rehabilitation, vocational training, and psychoeducational interventions?

Since most of us remember a question we wanted to ask only after we've left the doctor's office, we advise family members to keep a running list of questions that may occur to them about their relative's illness and treatment. These can then be raised during a subsequent consultation.

EVALUATING PROSPECTIVE "HELPERS"

Each professional and each facility attempt to practice "state of the art" psychiatry. Nevertheless, since the family members will almost certainly come into contact with or have to choose among various professionals and agencies, they need general guidelines for evaluating the adequacy of the treatment being offered. This involves, to a certain extent, learning to look past immediate outcome to a planful approach to ongoing service. Uneducated about the limits of current psychiatric knowledge, families are likely to evaluate therapeutic competence on the grounds of whether their relative gets well quickly. This often leads to fruitless "doctor shopping," as unrealistic expectations continue to be unmet. On the other hand, families should not be expected to accept interminable continuation of an unsuccessful plan of action. Rather, they can be taught to request and expect a clear proposal for treatment that includes strategies to cope with various contingencies that may arise (including, for example, medication side effects, lingering psychotic symptoms, and anergia).

Families can also learn to search out professionals who work comfortably and openly with families. Educating families so that they have a common language with which to converse with professionals and helping them to know what questions to ask facilitate this evaluative process. We suggest that families might want to ask (in addition to the questions already raised) some or all of the following questions in evaluating prospective therapists for their ill relative:

1) How do you view the confidentiality issue? Would you be willing to consult with us about diagnosis, medication, future planning? How long would it take to get an appointment? Are you available by phone?

   (*Professionals who use confidentiality inappropriately to avoid working with families will probably engender much frustration, which may, in fact, outweigh whatever good they might do with the patient.*)

2) What theoretical model of my relative's illness do you espouse? What do you believe to be the role of genetics? Environment? What do you believe is the family's role in bringing this illness about? What do you believe should be the family's role in rehabilitation?

   (*Families can learn to look for "buzz words" like "early mother-child relationship," "communication dysfunction," "intrapsychic conflicts," which may indicate that this therapist is likely to subtly or directly blame family members for the illness in their midst.*)

3) What is your view of a psychoeducational approach for our relative? For us? Would you object to our reading about our relative's illness? Would you provide or suggest reading material? Would you help us understand and apply what we have read?

   (*Professionals who need to mystify the illness by keeping the family away from educational materials are, in our view, either insecure about their own knowledge or unwilling to view the family as active partners in the rehabilitation effort.*)

4) Do you know about the National Alliance for the Mentally Ill? Its local affiliate? What do you think of it?

   (*Professionals who are still unaware of the existence of family support groups or who are negative about them are less likely to be conversant with and sympathetic to the needs of families.*)

5) What is your training and experience in working with the chronically mentally ill and their families?

(Sometimes less experienced therapists are to be preferred to more experienced ones; they often have more energy, enthusiasm, and a fresher outlook. On the other hand, experience in having learned from families what works and what doesn't can be invaluable. What is probably to be avoided most is a therapist who has experience or training which leads him or her to take a strictly family systems or antimedical orientation to psychotic disorders, as well as one whose medical bias is so strong that psychosocial rehabilitation is not considered.)

6) What procedures are available to us if we are dissatisfied with the service provided?

(We suggest that families evaluate the apparent comfort or defensiveness with which the prospective therapist answers this question.)

These six questions are for all of us to consider. Also, how do we, within our own practices or agencies, help families and patients become better at choosing and evaluating mental health services?

COMMUNICATING COOPERATIVELY

A more difficult side of helping family members work with professionals is helping them cope with their anger, resentment, frustration and skepticism in such a way that it does not perpetuate their (or their ill relative's) alienation from the treatment system. Not only must professionals be sensitive to the family's plight, but the family must learn to be sensitive to the predicament in which even the most open-minded clinician finds himself or herself when confronted by a hostile, confrontive, negativistic family member. The style with which family members and professionals communicate with each other is as important as the substance.

The clinician can help by pointing out the limits in our knowledge of psychiatric disorders and by sharing with the family his or her own frustration about diagnostic uncertainty, the limited efficacy of treatment, and the very real gaps in funding and services. Allowing the family to ventilate anger and admitting that even the most knowledgeable and well-intentioned clinicians can make errors also help. Reflecting feelings in a nondefensive way may be of value, as in the following exchange:

PARENT: (bitterly) He keeps getting more and more medicine, but he's not getting any better!

CLINICIAN: It sounds like you're angry with me and think I should be doing something differently.

PARENT: I'm just frustrated, that's all. Shouldn't he be getting better by now?

CLINICIAN: I'm frustrated, too, because this medicine has worked well in the past and I'm not sure why it's not working now. My plan was to give this a good therapeutic trial for a couple more weeks before we try a different one. Can you stick it out, or would you like us to get another psychiatrist to take a look and see if he can give us some other ideas?

PARENT: No, that's OK, I guess. I just wasn't sure if you knew it wasn't working. We're just so worried.

CLINICIAN: I know. I'm worried, too, but we haven't run out of things to try yet, so don't give up. The waiting is the hard part for all of us, isn't it?

One innovative approach to sensitizing families to the professional's position is to hold a workshop, moderated by an experienced family member and a clinician, in which families and professionals share what has been helpful and unhelpful in their contact with each other. We suggest that this be arranged so that families and clinicians who have *not* worked directly with each other are brought together. In this setting, generic communications about the kinds of behaviors that therapists find frustrating in family members and that family members find frustrating in therapists can be received with a minimum of personalization or defensiveness. Our own experience (Rockland County, NY, "Bridging the Gap" Conference, 1983) indicates that both families and clinicians find such a session highly enlightening and useful.

NEGOTIATING INSTITUTIONS

Negotiating the mental health bureaucracy presents a formidable challenge to families, who are often maximally stressed and disorganized at just the time when important decisions must be made. The treatment team should ensure that the family is helped to get through this maze. Specifically, the following points, at least, should be covered:

1) When and where is inpatient treatment appropriate?
2) What are the admissions procedures (both voluntary and involuntary)?
3) What financial aid is available? How does one apply?
4) What are the roles of the psychiatrist, team social worker, primary therapist, nursing staff? With whom should the family communicate about various issues that can be expected to arise?
5) What agency (or agencies) are available for follow-up care? What are the procedures for contacting them? Who has responsibility for making these contacts — staff, patient, or family?
6) What local, state, and federal agencies play a watchdog, advocacy or ombudsman function for the mentally ill and/or their families? How and under what circumstances should they be contacted?

Again, this material can be offered to groups of families with good result.

We in the mental health business are so used to the "alphabet soup" which we are fed daily that it is easy to lose sight of how confusing and inscrutable the system appears to outsiders. When conversing with families it is best to use whole names (Office of Vocational Rehabilitation) rather than abbreviations (O.V.R.). It is useful to outline steps to be taken slowly and carefully, giving the family a written "crib sheet" to refer to when they get home and can't remember what you've said. (It also helps to realize that in their shoes you wouldn't remember it all when you got home either!) Don't forget to inform families about waiting lists and lag times between application for services or funds and receipt.

COMMUNITY ADVOCACY

The mental health system comprises only one part of the patient's and family's environment. Advocacy on behalf of the ill relative may go far beyond working with professionals.

John is a 24-year-old, passive, withdrawn schizophrenic man. He lives with his parents in a middle-class residential suburb of a mid-sized city where he enjoys walking up and down the streets, speaking briefly with children whom he sees playing outside. He has no history of aggressive or sexual behavior and does nothing more than exchange a few words with the children; however, he is disheveled, lumbering, and awkward, which frightens several of the adults who know he has had some kind of "mental problems." They will not allow their children to play outside when he approaches. Two of them have called the police to complain about his "loitering" and trespassing.

The mentally ill person who lives in the community may be stigmatized and discriminated against not only by neighbors, but by schools, merchants, police, employers, and landlords, among others. Families often request guidance concerning whether, when, and how to get involved when conflict between the patient and members or agencies of the community arise. We generally use a problem-solving approach, with a focus on helping the family answer the following questions:

1) Can the patient successfully handle the problem alone?
2) How negative would the outcome be without intervention? (This is essentially a de-catastrophizing question, designed to help the family separate the practical aspects from the emotional ones.)
3) Is successful intervention possible, given the family's knowledge, resources, time and energy?
4) Is the effort of intervening worth the cost in terms of time, energy, and frustration?

John's mother decides to intervene in the situation with the neighbors described above because she feels that John's routine would be badly disrupted if she did not (leaving her with more of a burden for filling his time) and because intervening would not require a large investment of time or energy. The first complainant refuses to talk with her, but the second is at least polite. John's mother explains about John's illness, emphasizes that he is not dangerous, and conveys that he seeks only a smile and a greeting before moving on. The woman, faced with a mother like herself, softens, and agrees to make an effort to get to know John so she can assess for herself what he is like. Neither she nor any other neighbor (surprisingly) makes any further calls to the police about John.

For some family members it is a short step from speaking to a neighbor about one's son to speaking to a local civic organization about many mothers' ill sons and daughters. Social and political advocacy becomes an outlet for the intense frustration generated by the conflict between the need to help the ill person and the realities of the illness. As much as families wish they could cure, protect, and provide for their ill loved one, in reality there is a limit to how much improvement in the quality of his or her life they alone can generate. In our experience, those who become involved in advocacy activities tend to be those who are most realistic about their own relatives. They have stopped trying to fix what they cannot fix (for the most part) and have turned their attention to improving the situation for others as much as for their own family member. Since we believe that for many people advocacy activities result in greater self-esteem, a sense of accomplishment, and diminution of helplessness, we recommend that clinicians educate families about the opportunities for advocacy and the ways to begin to get involved.

Opportunities for involvement include writing letters or articles for local press about misrepresentation of the mentally ill in the media, impending legislation involving funding of services for the mentally ill, or other pertinent issues. Another route involves joining a local zoning board (with respect to housing issues), school board (to advocate for the special educational needs of the mentally ill), community service advisory board, or mental health association. Becoming conversant with legislative issues that affect the mentally ill and active in working towards constructive change presents another avenue for investment of energy.

Is there a conflict of interest problem for the professional who encourages advocacy efforts?

> A mother mentions to the clinician that her son, a state hospital patient, is an avid swimmer. The clinician tells her that, although there is a pool on the state hospital campus, there is no allocation for salaries to staff it so it remains unused. Observing her frustration and annoyance, he is tempted to suggest that she contact her legislator, but isn't sure if doing so would be "out of line."

When it comes to funding services, providers and families are natural allies. Further, offering information and education about options is different from urging, coercing, or demanding. We believe it is possible to make relatives aware of advocacy possibilities because of the value such activity might have for them, as well as for the patient, even if it may benefit one's own institution or agency. Collegial consultation can help resolve whatever ethical dilemmas may arise in an individual case.

Of course, advocacy is not for everyone. Families who are coping with a first or second psychotic episode are usually far too pained and disorganized to consider anything beyond their relative's current care and treatment. There are others who prefer the more passive, traditional doctor-patient role relationship in which they accept what they are told, do what they are asked, and maintain the comforting illusion that the physician is omniscient if not omnipotent. We suggest that the clinician respect this position. After all, advocacy should not be simply another burden that family members feel they must bear. The most likely candidates, in our experience, are those family members who seem to have an abundance of energy (that may surface as anger at the system or frustrated overinvolvement with the ill person). For these people, advocacy efforts may successfully redirect their energy into more productive channels.

FACILITATING ACCESS TO OTHER FAMILIES

While we have alluded previously to various ways in which family support groups can be of value, it is in this area of fostering competent consumerism and enhancing advocacy skills that these groups have one of their greatest benefits. This is particularly true of local affiliates of the National Alliance for the Mentally Ill (NAMI), which are free-standing and, as such, not wedded to a particular agency or approach. The value of NAMI to families is attested to by the growth of its membership, which has been so rapid since its establishment in 1979 that any estimate is immediately out of date (although the number is somewhere in the tens of thousands nationwide). With chapters in each of the 50 states and counterparts in Canada, the United Kingdom and Australia (at least), this organization provides emotional support, educational opportunities, and political advocacy for its members. Supportive professionals can make their own jobs immeasurably easier by referring families to the nearest NAMI affiliate (see Appendix B).

Many professionals are wary of self-help groups and threatened by the consumer orientation they teach their members. And indeed, members are likely to be far less passive and far more involved in treatment and advocacy than nonmembers. They are likely to be as wary of the professional as the professional is of them. Those who prefer the family to be docile, dependent, or uninvolved may find that the educated, questioning, involved family presents quite a challenge. However, the self-help group's capacity to counter helplessness, defeatism, isolation, and loneliness more than compensates for whatever initial tension is provoked between consumer and professional. The group's ability to teach families the jargon they will need to communicate effectively with therapists is but one of many ways in which the family-therapist relationship is actually facilitated by membership. In reality, an informed family member acts as the therapist's eyes and ears, as well as ensuring, by his or her very presence, that the treatment plan will be carefully thought out. Indeed, most of us organize our ideas a bit more clearly when our work is being observed than when it is not.

Within consumer groups, families learn about what is available for their relative locally. They become more adept at locating supportive professionals and programs appropriate for their ill family member. They become active allies in fighting reduction of funding to needed programs for the chronically mentally ill. In addition, by relating to other families' experiences they become more realistic about the illness, and the intensity of their wish for a "quick fix" diminishes. They are thereby enabled to work more productively with professionals.

Rather than simply notifying the family of the group's existence, the professional should, we suggest, go farther – by asking the family members' permission to have a NAMI member contact them, by introducing them to a NAMI family, by getting their agreement to attend a meeting and then following through by discussing with them their impressions, or even by accompanying them to a meeting.

If there is no local affiliate, agency-based groups can be started with the hope that they may become free-standing in time, although we have found that families' natural dependence on professionals for leadership makes this goal somewhat difficult to attain. If this strategy is tried, we suggest making the professional's regular involvement clearly time-limited (perhaps phasing it out gradually) with lots of encouragement for members to get to know each other outside of group time. The focus should be on teaching group development, leadership, and public relations skills that will enable the group to function autonomously when the professional withdraws from the leadership role.

In rural areas, a mutual support group may not be feasible. In this situation, a family who is new to the system can be put in touch with a more experienced family known to the clinician or the clinician's colleagues.

Mrs. H. was faced with the first psychiatric admission of her 20-year-old son, who was acutely psychotic and suicidal. The community psychiatric nurse who had facilitated admission to the nearest psychiatric unit (which was 45 miles away) felt that Mrs. H. needed far more support than she herself could provide. With Mrs. H.'s permission, she contacted Mrs. K., the parent of a schizophrenic daughter who had been ill for over nine years. Mrs. K. had been quite successful in learning about mental illness, coping with her daughter's behavioral problems, making use of her own social support system, and working cooperatively with professionals. Mrs. K. called Mrs. H. They began a relationship which was instrumental in helping Mrs. H. negotiate the treatment system effectively, as well as begin the process of emotional healing that is so important to families of the chronically mentally ill.

George Albee (1981) has proposed the following equation for psychological dysfunction:

$$\frac{\text{Incidence of}}{\text{Dysfunction}} = \frac{\text{Stress} + \text{Constitutional Vulnerabilities}}{\text{Social Supports} + \text{Coping Skills} + \text{Competence}}$$

Either reducing the numerator or increasing the denominator will have a positive impact on the risk for dysfunction. In this chapter we have focused on increasing the denominator through linking families with an indigenous mutual support system and teaching them the skills needed to successfully advocate for themselves and their ill relative within the complex professional mental health system.

III

PROFESSIONAL DILEMMAS

10

WORKING WITH
DIFFICULT FAMILIES

We have presented a framework for helping families of the
mentally ill which emphasizes the importance of a working
alliance and assumes the family's ability to establish this
alliance. In our experience, most families are more capable
than is often presumed by mental health professionals. However, some families present special challenges to the profes-
sional-family relationship. In this chapter we describe some
particularly problematic families, families with whom we had
great difficulty or were unable to establish a working alliance.
We offer these examples in order to illustrate our own limitations and to place our recommendations into perspective. At
any given point in time many families may bear some resem-
blance to these cases. Most families experience acute adjustment problems in response to their relative's illness (for
example, anger at the therapist, denial, excessive anxiety and
guilt), but these usually resolve with time and supportive intervention. Other families have much more persistent difficulties that constitute major impediments to working constructively with them. The latter are the focus of this chapter.
Recognizing these families is essential to maintaining a viable
professional perspective, preventing burnout and avoiding
overgeneralization to other families, thus producing the common avoidance of families by professionals.

A DISENGAGED FAMILY

Mr. D., a 58-year-old man, had spent over two years in a VA hospital recovering from a major depressive episode during which he shot himself with a hunting gun. He was left with multiple physical sequelae of the suicide attempt and, in addition, suffered another period of severe depression while hospitalized for which he received a course of electroconvulsive therapy. During his hospitalization his wife had refused to visit and now she refused to take him home. In her view, he had "ruined our [the family's] lives." Staff's attempts to convince her that he was ill and needed her, that he was ready to be discharged, that she was responsible for him, and that there was no good alternative to home placement failed to sway her. Finally, her daughter convinced her to seek counseling for herself.

Several issues relevant to her active disengagement emerged during treatment. The first was guilt. Despite Mr. D.'s significant weight loss over a period of several months and his almost continual complaints that he was sleeping poorly, Mrs. D. failed to seek help for her husband's condition. He had had episodes of depression in past years, each of which had spontaneously resolved; quite naturally, she expected this one would too.

In addition to feeling intensely guilty, Mrs. D. was fearful about the future. If she was unable to predict and prevent one catastrophic suicide attempt, how could she cope with the possibility that it might happen again? If she were to let down her guard enough to let him back into her life, how would she survive if he succeeded in killing himself next time? No one on the hospital staff had ever spoken to her about her husband's illness, except to say that he was depressed. No one had educated her about warning signs and strategies for intervention.

Finally, it became clear that Mr. D.'s illness was only one of several stressors for his wife. Their youngest daughter, who had psychotic episodes, lived at home. Mrs. D. lived in a big, old farmhouse in an isolated rural area. She would have liked to move into town, but her son fought her attempts to sell the farmhouse. She worked a fulltime job to support the family and couldn't imagine how she would provide supervision for her husband while she was at work. Following several months of treatment in which these issues were addressed, Mrs. D. agreed to take her husband home on a trial basis, although not without serious reservations and much unresolved anger at him and at treatment personnel.

The "disengaged family" is the most common problem reported by family clinicians. These families appear to "dump" their relative on the mental health system and refuse to accept further responsibility. Several reasons for this are illustrated in this case example. Unresolved conflicts, lack of attention to family members' needs and feelings by treatment staff, ignorance about the illness, and lack of a good community support system all contribute to the problem. Mrs. D was able to reengage when day treatment services, weekly (rather than monthly) mental health appointments, and 24-hour telephone availability were offered. In this way she was able to share responsibility for monitoring her husband's status and was able to receive much needed support for herself. In addition, inpatient staff would do well to support involvement at whatever level the family member can tolerate. Mrs. D., for example, had refused to visit her husband partly because she assumed that doing so would increase staff's pressure on her to take Mr. D. home. As is true with hostile families, the attitude "What can we do *for you?*" works better than "What are *you going to do* for the patient?"

A HOSTILE FAMILY

Peter and Mary S., the parents of a 20-year-old daughter, Marcia, with chronic schizophrenia, were upset with the care being provided Marcia by a local mental health clinic. They did not like her therapist, her psychiatrist, her medications, or any other aspect of her treatment. They attended a clinic educational workshop on schizophrenia, but this seemed only to further anger them. They frequently quoted and misquoted what was taught in order to argue with Marcia's therapist about her care. This pattern had been characteristic with every care provider over nearly all of the three years of Marcia's illness. They had repeatedly threatened to sue various agencies for negligence, had taken their daughter abruptly out of several programs, and managed to alienate almost every mental health professional with whom they had had contact. It was subsequently learned that they had had similarly antagonistic relationships with Marcia's teachers in junior and senior high school. Mr. S. had actually once punched a school guidance teacher while arguing about his daughter's poor progress in school. A review of her record indicated several apparently valiant attempts by clinicians to engage the family supportively, but none was successful.

Marcia was finally admitted to a special inpatient unit for young adults with chronic mental disorders. This program had a strong orientation toward working with families in a supportive and educational fashion. Marcia was passively compliant with the program, but complained frequently to her parents about her care. Her parents in turn complained to her therapist, to the unit chief, and to the director of the hospital. After several meetings with the therapist and unit chief in which the parents variously accused the hospital staff of incompetence, surreptitious medical experimentation at their daughter's expense, and insensitivity to their needs, they demanded her release. Most recently Marcia has been under the care of a private psychiatrist and her parents have been contemplating a lawsuit against the hospital and admitting physician.

In this case, it seemed clear to those caring for the patient that the parents were chronically distressed about their daughter's illness and were expressing their frustrations through hostility. We say this only after repeated attempts by sensitive, supportive, and experienced family counselors to engage them in a constructive manner. The parents seemed bent on maintaining their self-protective, hostile stance, and they usually managed to elicit a rejecting, guarded attitude from clinicians. Mrs. S. at times seemed mildly paranoid, and Mr. S. had had occasional legal problems due to minor altercations with others. These parental problems, although not diagnosed as mental disorders, undoubtedly contributed to the pattern of response.

In our experience the most common causes of a family's hostility are guilt or fear about the patient's illness, resistance to acceptance of the patient's chronic disability and the implications of this for their lives, and previous, negative experiences with the treatment system. Usually it is possible to overcome this hostility with patience and gradual efforts to understand the family's pain and to ally with them. It often helps to bring the feelings of guilt, fear, sadness, or despair out into the open by acknowledging that it is common for families to experience these feelings when faced with a chronically ill relative. However, a hostile family may be quick to interpret such comments as condescending or as trying to focus on them rather than on "the real problem," the patient. Similarly, one walks a fine line when having them discuss their past travails with other professionals. One must be empathic without reinforcing their negative distortions of the current situation or creating unrealistic expectations about yourself that may only lead to their further disappointment. The counselor needs to preserve sufficient professional distance in order to render objective advice and to provide feedback when their current, hostile behaviors may have a self-actualizing effect on those trying to help.

A MULTIPLE PATIENT FAMILY

This upper-middle-class family included a high achieving lawyer father, a stepmother with a paranoid personality disorder, three daughters of the father (ages 23, 17, and 14), and a son of the stepmother (age 16). The patient under our care was the 17-year-old daughter, who suffered from a schizoaffective disorder. The oldest daughter carried the diagnoses of manic-depressive illness and borderline personality disorder, and the youngest daughter had made several relatively minor suicide threats and was flaunting a sexual relationship with an older man before her parents.

Family meetings were attempted with the entire family together and with the parents alone. In the meetings with the entire family, the stepmother dominated, arguing with most statements made by the family clinician and verbally attacking the patient and her father. The father remained quiet, but was obviously intimidated by his wife and typically ended the sessions with a depressive review of what a mess things were at home. The two older daughters were supportive of each other in the face of their stepmother's criticisms, but the youngest daughter openly argued with both of her sisters and with her stepmother. In meetings with only the parents, the wife would alternate between sharp criticisms of her husband for being "weak" or insensitive and guilt-ridden statements about her own failings as a mother. She perceived most statements by her husband or the family clinician as critical and would immediately assume a defensive stance. The husband would behave much as he did in the larger family sessions. Attempts to educate the parents about manic-depressive illness, schizoaffective disorder, and treatment were met by derisive comments by the stepmother directed at the father, blaming his genes for the daughters' problems (and by implication absolving herself of blame), and by a depressive, guilt-ridden response by the father.

After several fruitless months of work with this family, the treatment team decided to focus only on individual psychotherapy in conjunction with pharmacotherapy for the patient. Although the family conflicts continued, the clinical conditions of both older daughters stabilized and they were able to work to support themselves after leaving their parents' home. In this family, the psychopathology of the members combined to overwhelm them as well as the family clinician.

When more than one family member is mentally ill, the clinician must attempt to ally with the healthy or strong members or at least with the healthier sides of the impaired members. This can sometimes be accomplished more effectively by working with individual family members rather than with the family as a group. The goal is to maximize the healthier members' ability to cope with family problems. It may be necessary to separate family members from each other rather than engage them in further confusing and chaotic group interactions. This strategy, in turn, can add new stability to the family situation and thus reduce stress that leads to maladaptation among other family members. It pays to meet as many family members as possible in order to recognize where strengths lie in the family. It may be with a grandparent or older sibling, persons frequently excluded from the usual patient-parents or patient-spouse family sessions. Once identified, these relatives may need encouragement and support from the family clinician to enhance their capacity to help their less functional relatives cope more effectively.

A HIGH DENIAL FAMILY

Mr. and Mrs. D. had a 22-year-old son, Paul, with a developmental disorder characterized by multiple physical defects and psychosis. They had two other sons, both apparently normal. Paul was admitted to a long-term care hospital after several briefer hospitalizations in more acute facilities. Paul lived with his parents, but was becoming increasingly unmanageable because of the progressive nature of his psychosis (including violent outbursts), his size, and his parents' increasing age. Despite the many years of obvious disability and abnormal development, Mr. and Mrs. D. maintained that Paul was really not much different from their other boys and given the right environment he would "come around." Paul's physical and mental limitations, prognosis, and recommended treatment were repeatedly explained to them, but they held steadfastly to the belief that he could be cured. They frequently criticized his treatment programs, past and present, and made numerous appointments with the hospital director. Against the recommendations of the treatment team, they took him out of the hospital and back to their home. Within a month he had been rehospitalized after yet another fight with his father. Paul actually seemed content in the hospital, and with this latest hospitalization his parents were beginning to say that he might be better off "for the time being" in the hospital. This couple was struggling to hold on to prior expectations about their son. Although their denial was marked, it should be noted that repeated attempts at educating them about his problems, many supportive family sessions, and repeated failures to maintain him at home seemed to be helping them accept his limitations.

As we know, denial defends against painful or unacceptable reality. The painful reality of a chronically disabled child can overwhelm any parent's defenses, and efforts to help parents accept this reality may require considerable time and patience. It helps to encourage them to recount their expectations for their child prior to the onset of the illness and to discuss their hopes for an eventual "cure." This discussion often allows them to express their feelings of sadness and grief over the loss of what might have been. Some families find it helpful to assume an "as if" attitude. They can discuss the patient's disability "as if" it will be long-term, while still retaining their unrealistic expectations that the patient will recover fully. They then can develop plans "as if" the illness were chronic without having to come face-to-face immediately with this reality, an admission which in turn might paralyze their actions. With time, as realistic options become apparent and they begin to recognize that reality is not as bad as their worst fears, they may find it easier to drop the "as if" position. Families should not be pushed into giving up their denial prematurely (or entirely), but can be helped to adapt in spite of their need to protect themselves from the harsh reality of chronic mental illness.

AN IMPOVERISHED, DISORGANIZED, CRISIS-ORIENTED FAMILY

Mrs. G., an unemployed single mother and grandmother, lived with her 25-year-old mentally retarded, psychotic son, her 20-year-old borderline retarded, psychotic daughter, and her 5-year-old and 3-year-old grandchildren, the offspring of another daughter who had deserted them. Mrs. G. herself had only a sixth grade education, and she quite understandably felt overwhelmed by her situation. Both of her children would become aggressive at home when psychotic, and at times there was considerable concern for the safety of the grandchildren. Both daughter and son were frequently in and out of the state hospital, and the son was involved in a program for mentally retarded adults.

Numerous professionals and agencies had contact with the patients and their mother, including both patients' therapists (two separate mental health clinics), the state hospital, the staff at the day program for mentally retarded adults, the Department of Social Services, and the Child Protective Agency. Mrs. G. would not or could not leave her home to come to meetings with professionals or agencies, so various social workers had contact with her. However, they reported that she always appeared overwhelmed at home and was seemingly unable to absorb their information or recommendations. Attempts by a family clinician to engage her at home were similarly unproductive. Whenever things felt out of hand, her response was to give both her children increasingly higher doses of prescribed neuroleptics. For both of the patients, these high doses produced increased confusion and lethargy, and at times contributed to a highly disorganized psychotic state. This in turn interfered with their participation in day treatment programs and sometimes led to rehospitalizations.

All service providers concurred that the major path of intervention was to work toward eventual placement of the ill son and daughter outside the home. Foster care was being considered for the grandchildren, but the impression was that Mrs. G. might be able to provide them a loving, viable home if the other two were not at home. As of this writing, the son spends two days per week in "respite care" at a group home for mentally retarded adults and attends a day program five days per week. The daughter is again in the state hospital.

In encountering this situation, we might mobilize as many resources for the family as possible: home aides, church volunteers, extended family, and so on. Also, when attempting to help low IQ persons or persons under extreme environmental stress, one needs to provide very concrete, behavioral instructions at a pace that avoids overwhelming the person. Flooding the family with information, ideas, or assistance may have just the opposite of the desired effect.

A VIP FAMILY

Harry S. was a 26-year-old man with manic-depressive illness. His father, president of an international conglomerate, spent most of his time flying to various parts of the world in connection with his business. His mother lived at the family home in a major northeastern U.S. city. Harry's illness responded to lithium carbonate during his brief hospitalization, but he usually failed to comply with this treatment once he was out of the hospital. Because he traveled about the country on his parents' expense accounts, even when not manic, there was little continuity in his psychiatric care.

Most recently, Harry was admitted to a psychiatric hospital in California in a manic state, having spent several thousand dollars using his parents' credit cards. The primary therapist and family clinician requested a meeting with his parents. To the clinician's surprise, both parents agreed, though reluctantly, to fly to California for a "conference." The parents met first with the director of the hospital to introduce themselves and to inform him of their plans to meet with the hospital staff treating their son. In the meeting with the therapist and family clinician, they summarily rejected the need to discuss "family issues" that might be related to their son's behavior, insisting instead that Harry would eventually outgrow his adolescence. Against medical advice, they removed Harry from the hospital and took him back home to be seen by a psychiatrist who was a friend of the family. Harry recently sent a postcard from Africa to his former therapist at the California hospital; he was once again traveling "to find himself."

In this case an error was probably made in trying to move too quickly to discuss "family issues." This immediately put the parents in a defensive position and further mobilized their need (and considerable ability) to be in charge. In such circumstances, the family clinician can utilize the family's capacity for executive function by acting as the family consultant. The clinician may point out their options, always stressing that the decision ultimately rests with them. They are free to ask questions that will help in their decision process. The clinician's role becomes that of advisor, educator, collaborator.

A FAMILY DEPENDENT UPON
THE PATIENT'S ILLNESS

Charles was a 21-year-old man with chronic schizophrenia who lived with his parents. He had been ill since age 16 and had been hospitalized eight times in five years. His father worked as a part-time janitor and his mother was a housewife. A pattern had become apparent relating his illness relapses and conflict between his parents, who had separated three times in ten years and who were, as they said, "barely able to stand each other." Charles' hospitalizations typically occurred at times of increased conflict between his parents and when marital separations seemed imminent. At these times, he stopped taking his antipsychotic medication, which only further added to the parental conflict, with each parent blaming the other for "making him sick." However, once he was hospitalized, the parents would declare a "truce" so that they could be available to him.

Although they willingly attended a class on schizophrenia and its treatment, including a discussion of the relationship of stress at home to relapse, and intellectually acknowledged that their marital problems seemed to exacerbate his illness, they made no sustained effort to break this cycle. The family clinician recommended marital counseling for them, interpreting their possible investment in Charles' relapses to save their marriage, and advised them and Charles that he might be better served by moving to a group home. The parents accepted the recommendation for marital counseling but failed to follow through, and rejected the idea of Charles' leaving home, expressing instead guilt and a renewed commitment to "make things right" for him. In the process of these discussions, the mother also revealed that they were partially dependent on his SSI checks for family support. Hence, in this case the parents were both psychologically and materially invested in his illness and resistant to any interventions that might disrupt this arrangement.

How does one intervene with this type of family? Perhaps the most difficult aspect is overcoming one's own sense of disapproval of their apparent exploitation of the patient. Such feelings further detract from one's ability to relate to them and hence to affect how they deal with the patient. It can help to start by recognizing that they do care about the patient and that they are not *simply* exploiting his illness for their benefit. If one can develop an appreciation of this positive aspect of their relationship with the patient, it will be easier to empathize with them. They may respond to this and begin to ally themselves with the family clinician. Gradually they may be able to disengage some of their self-interests from the patient's and find alternative ways to meet their own needs. Finally, even if little change can be effected, such a family may be better than no family at all, and we must refrain from viewing a maintenance of the status quo as the worst possible outcome of our interventions. Certainly patients can be exploited by landlords, residential care facilities, institutions, and denizens of the streets. A family that exploits the patient's illness may be more benign than these alternatives.

A MALICIOUS FAMILY

Marie, a 28-year-old woman, was admitted for her first psychiatric hospitalization with a paranoid psychosis and depression. She believed that she was going to die as a result of "a contract placed on her head" by her brother-in-law and that the hospital and staff were not what they appeared to be, but rather, an elaborate deception. She was convinced that she would be murdered in the hospital, perhaps by poison in the medication. She, therefore, refused all medication and eventually took it only on an involuntary basis.

At the time of admission her husband gave a history of relatively acute psychotic decompensation in response to "kidding" of the patient by his brother regarding the family business. However, two weeks after hospitalization, her two sisters flew in from another part of the country and expressed concern that the husband and brother were attempting to harm the patient. They gave a different history. The patient had led an isolated life since age 15, was always passive and withdrawn, and had married at age 17 to escape a foster home. Although not previously treated for a mental disorder, she had probably been psychotic intermittently for some time. They believed that the husband and brother-in-law were indeed conspiring against the patient in order to gain full control of the family business by having her declared incompetent.

Shortly thereafter, the husband requested that the patient be transferred for treatment in another city, but this request was refused by the patient and her therapist. The sisters maintained contact with the patient, but had to return home. Two months later, the husband filed for divorce and contested her control of the business. The patient eventually responded to a combination of antipsychotic and antidepressant medications and psychotherapy. She was discharged to live in a group home, and secured legal counsel to help with the divorce and business problems.

In this case an alliance was possible between the sisters and the treatment team, although this was limited by distance. Obviously such an alliance was not possible with the patient's husband. This demonstrates the importance of finding out where the supports lie in the family and capitalizing on them.

These examples illustrate the array of highly resistant or problematic families that the family clinician may encounter.

In retrospect, these cases may seem extreme or obvious, but for most of them the situation was not so clear initially. This is always the clinician's dilemma. How can we differentiate at the outset between these families and others who will prove to be more responsive to our efforts? There are some things that can help in clarifying the situation. For example, the family's history of dealing with previous crises and problems and their use of supports and resources at such times can be useful in anticipating their capacity to deal with their current problems related to the patient's illness and to make use of the family clinician's services. Disorganized or highly conflicted families often lack the resources to engage in family counseling effectively, even though these families may be the most in need.

Nonetheless, we know of no sure way to predict how a family will respond to attempts to engage them. Early unworkability in a family is not necessarily predictive. Only long-term involvement, or at least intermittent contact with family members over a period of time, can settle this issue. Therefore, we recommend proceeding on the assumption that the family has the capacity to form a working alliance. The most serious risk is that of omission, that is, the failure to attempt an alliance with the family. Too often we hear families described by staff as "hostile," "pathological," "too involved," or "not interested" on the basis of one or two interactions. The decision not to work with them follows all too soon from this often erroneous premise. We can think of no case in which failed attempts to engage the family actually harmed either the patient or family. If the decision is made to terminate because of the types of problems described in this chapter, every effort should be made to end on good terms and to let the family members know that you are still concerned and interested in how they are doing. Periodic, brief contacts with them (for example, by phone) may keep the door open for their return for help at a time when they are better prepared to accept this.

These problematic families do pose a risk to the therapist. Each of us must have the capacity to recognize when our best efforts have not been effective and when it is time to desist. Indeed, we have a responsibility to ourselves, our patients, and their families to admit when we can no longer work effec- tively with them. We may refer the family to another clinician for a "fresh" start or simply acknowledge that at this time fur- ther attempts to help the family probably will not be useful. Sharing our frustrations with our peers can help to maintain a realistic perspective and prevent professional burnout. Tak- ing care of these feelings in ourselves also reduces unneces- sary demoralization in the family and further exacerbation of their negative feelings about professionals or themselves. At some future point they may be more capable of accepting support from the counselor.

Most families can develop a working alliance with the clini- cian, but there are always some who cannot. While these families are less common than sometimes thought, the clini- cian must be prepared to recognize them. In our opinion, every family deserves a chance, and every clinician has the right and responsibility to say "enough is enough."

11

BIASES, LOYALTIES, AND CONFLICTS

There exist a number of personal and institutional blocks to working with families in the ways we have described. Few of us are personally prepared to do so by virtue of our previous training and experiences. Since the role of family clinician is relatively new, there is still great potential for overlap of function and staff conflict. In this chapter, we examine some of the problems facing clinicians who are preparing themselves to engage in supportive psychoeducational work with families.

OVERCOMING NEGATIVE
FEELINGS TOWARDS FAMILIES

By the time we begin clinical work, many of us have already developed unhelpful attitudes towards families of the chronically mentally ill. Clinicians who have been trained within a strict medical model tend to see the person with the illness in a vacuum. Their goals are to reduce the psychotic symptoms as much and as quickly as possible, and then to return the person to his or her environment. Often little thought is given to how his residual symptoms affect and are affected by those around him. They confine their instructions and discussions to the ill person and communicate infrequently with the family. Further, they rarely initiate conversations with families, but wait for families to contact them. Their attitude towards families is one of benign neglect. Clinicians so trained also tend to have the most difficulty with the confidentiality issue and tend to view their responsibility in such a way that they are reluctant to share any data without clear and concrete permission from the patient.

> The parent of a 20-year-old schizophrenic inpatient inquired about what medication her son was supposed to take during his weekend home visit. The charge nurse refused to tell her and also refused to ask the patient, who was standing nearby, whether it would be all right to tell her.

> The daughter of a 58-year-old paranoid schizophrenic woman inquired as to whether her mother still had delusional ideas about being poisoned by the family. She was reluctant to take her mother home without knowing what to expect. The clinician refused to tell her on the grounds that the patient's communications were privileged.

These issues are not easy ones to resolve, but successful treatment of the chronically mentally ill (and, indeed, of the chronically physically ill) is dependent upon sensitive awareness of the effect of the illness on the patient's social system. The medical model, narrowly applied, leaves many of us unprepared to approach illness in its larger context.

On the other hand, models which have embedded the illness in an interpersonal context have, at least until quite recently, neglected the biological substrate and too often focused on the family as etiological agent. Typically, most nonmedical mental health professionals come out of graduate school with these models firmly entrenched in mind. Subtly, or not so subtly, they are prepared to view the family as a major part of the problem.

In sum, most of us are ill prepared by our education and training to view the family as a valued ally in the treatment of chronic mental illness. Rarely have we read about, heard about, or discussed examples of adaptive family coping. Our training has been pathology-oriented. Clinical experiences are then viewed through the lenses that our education has provided. With selective perception, we fit the data to the model. Add to this the environmental causation approach that seems to pervade the folklore of our culture (who among us is unaware that the sins of teenagers are the fault of their parents), and it becomes clear that numerous biases stand in the way of effective work with families. Clinicians who prepare to work with the chronically mentally ill would do well to ferret out and reexamine the assumptions and models they have been taught to accept.

Not all of the negative views clinicians hold about such families can be explained this way, however. Rather, several aspects of the ways in which these families present themselves can reinforce negative stereotypes.

A family-oriented clinician was lecturing to a community group about schizophrenia. During the discussion period, one woman rose and in a confrontive manner inquired, "If my daughter is so sick, how come she remembers the words to every song she hears on the radio? I think she's just putting us and the doctors on." The clinician was aware of immediate tightness in the muscles of his stomach, shoulders, neck and face. His thoughts were, "Oh boy, here we go again! I'm in for the long haul now."

Anger and denial, two of the most common responses to recently diagnosed mental illness in the family, are also two of the most difficult for clinicians to tolerate. It is far from easy to remain empathic, undefensive and patient in the face of this kind of onslaught. It is tempting to view such a woman as unworkable. This was far from true, however, as this same woman provided some of the examples of adaptive coping we have used in this volume, although it took close to a year following the first contact to develop them. In fact, the very energy that the clinician had felt as an attack was later harnessed in the service of setting limits for her daughter, combatting stigma in her own milieu, and becoming involved in valuable advocacy issues.

Just as patients develop insight gradually, so do their families. Therefore, our task is to avoid responding impulsively on the basis of the initial hostile and defensive feeling we may have. The ability to "walk in their shoes," to feel their pain and confusion, and to see the adaptive potential in their defenses constitutes the most potent antidote.

Another part of the clinician's response to the woman in this example involves the discomfort we have about "being in for the long haul." Just as psychotic symptoms wax and wane, the feelings and problems that family members bring to counseling sessions are rarely put to rest or solved completely. Rather, grief, overinvolvement, insight, coping skills, and isolation fluctuate over time. Sometimes a worsening in the patient's condition stimulates a deterioration in some aspect of family functioning. Sometimes an anniversary phenomenon, meeting a healthy age mate of the ill person, or a chance remark by an acquaintance can shake defenses that had appeared impenetrable.

> The parents of a 23-year-old schizophrenic, drug-abusing son were finally able, after a year's counseling, to move him out of the family home into an apartment of his own. Despite remaining involved in his laundry, shopping, and transportation needs, they at least had reclaimed some sense of privacy and ownership of their home. Four years later, following one of several inpatient stays, they built an apartment in their basement for him, and brought him home.

> A couple had worked diligently to understand and accept the angry, resentful feelings of their 34-year-old daughter towards her 31-year-old mentally ill brother. Most of the time they did well, but at Christmas they became hurt and furious because she requested that they visit her (and her husband and son)

for part of the day so that she would not have to come home and be in the company of her brother. They told her that if she couldn't accept her brother, then she could do without them as well. This incident caused a rift that took months to heal, and seemed like an "instant replay" of scenes that had occurred ten years previously.

The physician father of a 30-year-old mentally ill woman was able to accept her and even to take pleasure in her job as a library aide, except when he ran into one or another of her ivy league college roommates. It seemed to him they were each happily married professional women. Each time he met one, he experienced a period of sadness lasting several days to several weeks.

The clinician who works with the chronically mentally ill and their families learns not to look for "cures" or even for permanent improvement in all areas of adaptation. Rather, a course studded with plateaus and even occasional setbacks is the norm. Thus, like work with the chronically or terminally physically ill, this endeavor requires a clinician who can find other sources of ego gratification beyond curing pathology. Clinicians who feel the need for closure, for termination of treatment following achievement of clear treatment goals, will inevitably find working with these families (and their ill relatives) draining and frustrating.

However, physical medicine offers an alternative way of viewing our work—the primary care role. Rather than viewing ourselves as specialists who diagnose, treat, and cure a particular illness, we might do well to see ourselves as "family doctors" of mental health. Were we to do so, we would expect return visits over the life of the family, sometimes for recurrences of old problems, sometimes for occurrences of new ones. We would expect to be able to "cure" certain of the ailments family members bring to us, but not others. In short, our goals would be to ameliorate problems as best we could when they arose. We would be satisfied to provide empathy and support when we had nothing more to offer. We would take it as evidence of faith in us when clients returned, not as evidence of treatment failure.

Dependency is another characteristic of these families which may stir up discomfort in clinicians. Medical practitioners have been trained for a directive, quasi-parental role and, by and large, handle it comfortably. However, most nonmedical clinicians who work with families have been trained in a humanistic, nondirective model which fails to prepare them for the role these families will thrust upon them. They are much more comfortable helping clients reach their own conclusions through nondirective interventions than they are in offering direct advice. The continual questions – "What should I do about this?" and "How should we handle that?" – may confuse and anger clinicians who feel that to answer out of their own intuitions or knowledge would be out of keeping with their role, or would not help the family learn to make independent decisions, or would be disrespectfully intrusive, or would be simply frightening (after all, one could be wrong!). They may even view frustrating these attempts to get advice as a therapeutic maneuver if they see the family's dependency as pathological.

We, however, see the family's dependency as quite normal. People come to experts (attorneys, accountants, physicians) to get advice. If a family requests advice on how to handle psychotic behavior and the clinician lacks knowledge or skills in that area, a referral is in order, rather than simply doing what one usually does in a nonpsychotic outpatient practice. We view families' reliance on our expertise as appropriate (although they often think we know more than we do) and their requests for advice and guidance as their right.

However, it is sometimes necessary to set limits with families, as with patients:

> The community mental health nurse in a rural
> county works with a manipulative demanding young
> adult chronic patient and his family. The parents

have a very difficult time setting limits for their son and have come to rely on her to do much of it for them. Recently, while in the hospital recuperating from surgery, she received a call from them requesting that she talk to their son and "calm him down." Needless to say, she felt inappropriately burdened and refused. Later she discussed with them under what specific circumstances she would accept being called when outside of the office.

We are not suggesting that the clinician must tolerate any and all dependency, but rather that it is useful to examine one's own feelings about this issue so that flexible guidelines that are suited to the needs of the population and consistent with the style of the clinician can be developed and communicated.

The final trait which seems to produce discomfort in clinicians is assertiveness on the part of family members.

The senior psychiatric resident treating a 28-year-old seriously psychotic young man decided to begin a trial of lithium carbonate and began by tapering the patient off of phenothiazines. The parents requested a consultation and asked about the basis for the decision, the long-term effects of lithium, and the possibility of maintaining phenothiazine treatment. The physician's first thoughts were, "I'm the doctor. I'm doing the best I can. Who are they to question my decision?" Later, in supervision, he was able to see that he had treated the family coldly because he was himself unsure of his decision and that he had lost rather than gained their trust.

Families who have been in the system long enough to know about its deficiencies and who know how little is actually known about mental illness can pose a threat to professionals who have not yet learned to accept these limitations in themselves. Insofar as treatment of the mentally ill remains as much art as science, it is not surprising that we should, from time to time, wonder if we are earning our keep. Knowledgeable family members can stimulate these uncertainties easily. However, we have found that knowledgeable consumers are often more tolerant of us than we are of ourselves. They know we don't have all the answers and can empathize with our uncertainty and frustration as we empathize with theirs. Unlike the dependent, naive family, these folks no longer expect us to be omnipotent. Rather, they provide us the opportunity to give up that unreasonable expectation of ourselves.

In sum, serious mental illness does not lend itself to a quick fix, nor can the issues which the illness generates in the family be easily and quickly resolved. Our own expectations and training biases, combined with the ways in which families approach us, can produce a host of uncomfortable feelings that may interfere with maintaining a supportive, patient posture. It is often easier to avoid or pathologize families than it is to join with them, sharing their burden of sadness and frustration and tolerating the very real limits in our capacity to make things better for them. Paradoxically, it is just this sort of sharing that family members report is most comforting and most helpful.

ROLE AMBIGUITY

Having overcome (at least for the most part) old biases and counterproductive attitudes, the family clinician is still faced with a host of practical problems relating to role definition. First is the question about whether the patient's primary therapist can function effectively as the family's clinician. On the plus side, the patient's therapist knows the patient best and can probably offer the most cogent advice on handling problems that may arise. In addition, such a strategy obviates concern over conflicting advice coming from different sources. On the minus side, the clinician must constantly guard against inappropriate breaches of confidentiality and may get caught in a bind when what is good for the patient (or what the patient wants) is not what is good for the family.

For example, how is the clinician to respond when the patient wants to live at home and the only alternative is an unstimulating board and care home, but the patient's presence seriously disrupts the lives of other family members? And what counsel should be offered to the spouse of a chronically ill person regarding separation or divorce when the patient will be adversely affected by separation, but the spouse will be adversely affected by continuation of the marriage? These dilemmas, far from easy to resolve on moral grounds alone, may be complicated by the clinician's mixed loyalty. In addition, of course, some patients will be opposed to their therapist's becoming involved with their family, despite the clinician's feelings that such involvement would be useful.

In our view there is no clear prescription for resolving these problems. Rather, they must be approached on a case by case basis, taking into account the preferences of the patient and of the family, the possibility of conflict of interest problems, and the clinician's intuitions about what would work. It may be helpful to discuss these choices openly with the patient and family prior to a decision, explaining the pros and cons of each model, so that the family will be able to make a thoughtful rather than an impulsive decision. Treatment teams can try to be flexible enough to support family work by the primary therapist when possible and to provide for referral when indicated. Of course, even when the primary therapist and family clinician are separate people, joint sessions with both therapists present can be held around specific agenda items when so desired. This arrangement allows for confidential discussions that may, in turn, lead to open negotiations.

Often the family clinician is thrust into the role of family advocate, both within the treatment team and with respect to the larger mental health system. This, too, can generate conflict.

A 20-year-old schizophrenic woman had recovered from an acute exacerbation of her illness and was medically ready to be discharged from the hospital.

The parents and siblings had painfully arrived at the decision that they did not want to take her back home to live. They had come to this decision with the help of the team social worker, who was left with the task of convincing the physician to hold the woman in hospital for the several weeks it would take to find even a marginally suitable alternative. The physician, under pressure to release the patient, suggested that the social worker try to convince the family that they must take her home, as she no longer needed to be in the hospital. The social worker refused. Her work with the family and her acceptance of the role of their spokesperson had brought her into conflict with her colleagues.

A clinician developed a supportive relationship with the family of a young man on an inpatient unit. The family felt dissatisfied both with the patient's treatment and with the lack of meaningful contact they felt they had with their son's psychiatrist. The clinician considered it her responsibility to inform the family of their right to a second opinion, to request a change of physician, to make use of various grievance mechanisms. At the same time, she was acutely aware of the effect this would have on her relationship with the attending psychiatrist and other staff.

A hospital psychiatric nurse found that her involvement with families had made her acutely sensitive to the gaps in housing, funding and involuntary commitment procedures. While, on the one hand, she wanted to become involved in advocacy issues, she wondered, on the other, whether she was taking on an inappropriate or conflicting role.

A staff member in an outpatient setting became aware that the chronically mentally ill were generally seen alone, for brief periods of time, at long intervals.

Having a mother with bipolar disorder himself, he felt strongly that the agency should have a family program of some kind and found himself advocating for one with a staff whose priorities were quite different and whose time was limited.

We view these conflicts as inevitable – the tension between patients' rights, families' rights, and institutional perogatives will always exist, causing some amount of role confusion and diffusion. One can only hope that the tension is creative, in that conflicts are dealt with openly and thoughtfully. Supervisory and peer relationships are critical here in terms of providing the objectivity that is essential to making a wise decision, as are personal flexibility, tolerance of ambiguity, and staying in touch with one's own comfort level with respect to these issues. Further, sensitivity to ethical issues should begin in graduate school, and ideally should continue in the professional setting, perhaps through formal seminars on the subject, or through informal discussions when issues arise. It is all too easy for institutions to encourage expediency over other values in decision-making, unless staff members feel free to question the assumptions underlying decisions.

INADEQUATE EXPERTISE

Working with these families requires a wide range of expertise and skills. One must have good knowledge of psychopathology – symptoms, medication, course, prognosis, etiological models, prognosis, and ancillary treatments. One must also have skills in behavioral management, problem-solving techniques and stress modification techniques. Further, one must have had enough contact with this population (either through reading or through clinical work) to understand the needs of families and their typical responses (both emotional and behavioral). Finally, one must have learned what advice to offer – which strategies are likely to work and which aren't. Lacking generic programs for training professionals to work with the chronically mentally ill and their families, it is rare than individual clinicians will have adequate expertise in each of these areas. More typically, various members of the treatment team are each involved with one aspect of the treatment plan (including, for example, medication, finances, referral to community programs, behavioral techniques). And, indeed, families are often referred from one to the other in their search for information and guidance. While this may be efficient from the institutional point of view, it is certainly not from the family's. While each of us is, quite rightly, hesitant to step outside of our own area of expertise, the solution involves expanding the expertise and job description of at least some staff members, who can then function as "family clinician for the chronically mentally ill." At present, these skills are acquired in a haphazard manner, if at all.

In this chapter we have illustrated some of the personal and institutional roadblocks encountered by clinicians who work with families of the chronically mentally ill. In many respects they are similar to those encountered in working with chronic patients themselves. Not all of us are suited for such work, and even those of us who are will confront these issues many times over. While we are unable to offer easy solutions, we do feel that most of the problems are resolvable when clinicians have access to a good peer support system and have set realistic, manageable goals for themselves. For us, the rewards are well worth the effort.

12

DEVELOPING A
FAMILY PROGRAM:
TIME TO BEGIN

Having discussed how therapists can develop supportive, educational relationships with families, we move, in this chapter, to a discussion of institutional issues. The first section addresses the nuts and bolts of developing a family-oriented program within an agency or institution. The second focuses on developing a training program at the graduate level for academic departments in psychiatry, psychology, social work, and nursing, as well as for institutions affiliated with such graduate departments. Finally, we address the professional rewards of working with families of the chronically mentally ill in the ways we have described.

SETTING PRIORITIES

Successful family programs involve substantial investment of staff time and energy and, as such, are dependent upon the institution's commitment to this work at the highest levels of administration. Until recently, programs for the chronically mentally ill have taken a back seat to programs for patients with more acute and less severe problems except in state hospital settings; even in state hospitals families have seldom been considered, except as part of the problem. Currently, both the federal government and many state governments have focused attention on the huge personal and economic loss this population represents and have made rehabilitation of the chronically mentally ill a priority. However, care of this population is still fragmented between state hospitals, private psychiatric units, outpatient mental health settings, transitional residence, day programs, and sheltered work settings. It remains up to each agency to decide how committed it will be to programs for the chronically mentally ill and to helping families cope with the chaos mental illness provokes in their lives. Often, the buck gets passed – inpatient staff members delegate family work to the therapists in transitional residences, who in turn try to pass this responsibility to primary therapists in outpatient mental health settings, who often feel the work should have been done by inpatient staffs. Social workers are uncomfortable talking to families about medication because they feel this should be done by the psychiatrist, but the psychiatrist is too busy to see the family at all. Family members, shuffled between agencies and therapists, are left with confusion, anger, and lingering hopelessness.

The problem is complicated by the reimbursement system which often funds direct service but neglects collateral contact or pays for it at an unreasonably low rate. Thus, administrators must not only decide that family work is a priority, but also figure out how to pay for it. Even highly motivated staff will be reluctant to develop a family program without the support and encouragement of the administration.

When support from administration is not forthcoming, it is still possible to begin a program on a small, experimental basis. Having a family education evening once a month is often possible, as is developing a brochure explaining policies and procedures to families. Administrators can often be convinced by feedback from families, evidence that the activity reduces other kinds of time spent, and the enthusiasm of their own staff members.

CONDUCTING ATTITUDE AND NEEDS ASSESSMENT

Once developing a family support program is acknowledged as a priority, the next step is to learn what the agency or institution is currently providing, how the service is viewed by families, and how staff and families view each other. We suggest instituting a survey of relatives (or a sample of relatives) of patients served by the agency. While a written questionnaire is the easiest method, telephone or face to face interviews (by an agency representative who has not worked with the family being polled) will generally yield more information and are preferable if time allows. In any case, the survey should cover the following areas:

1) What would you ideally like from professionals who are treating your relative in terms of education, information, guidance, and support?
2) What do you feel you have received from staff to date?
3) Has contact with staff been helpful to you; if so, in what ways?
4) Has contact with staff ever been unhelpful, frustrating, anger-provoking, or guilt-inducing? What happened?
5) Would you be interested in participating in short- or long-term educational seminars or support groups?
6) What general attitude towards families do you feel staff hold?

If families are asked during the interview to identify particular staff members with whom they have had contact, this information may be helpful in identifying which staff members have a particular talent in working with families and which may need additional training or supervision. On the other hand, family members may feel more comfortable in being candid if they don't have to worry about getting someone in trouble or having their complaints backfire through angry staff responses to their relative. The local National Alliance for the Mentally Ill (NAMI) group can be asked to provide consultation about this issue and about development of the survey instrument in general.

At the same time, staff members can be surveyed with respect to the following issues:

1) How often do you see or speak with families of patients with whom you work?
2) What is generally discussed?
3) Generally, do you initiate contact or do the families?
4) How often is family work part of the written service or treatment plan? When it is, what are its goals?
5) What do you believe to be the family's role in the development of chronic mental illness? In rehabilitation?
6) What resources for families (books, pamphlets, support groups) are you aware of? How often do you refer families to them?
7) What do you find to be the most difficult aspects of working with families? The most rewarding?
8) What skills do you feel you need to learn to enhance your competence in meeting the needs of families?
9) What do you believe families most want from clinicians?
10) How important do you feel family work is a) to yourself, b) to your supervisor, c) to agency administration?

Again, the tradeoff between the honesty that anonymity provides and the value of pinpointing staff members' strengths and weaknesses will have to be weighed. In any case, completion of the survey by all clinical staff members who work with the chronically mentally ill should be mandated in order to demonstrate to staff that work with families is an area of high priority and to provide a true picture of agency attitudes and activities.

SETTING THE STAGE

Generally, there is a large discrepancy between what professional staff think families want (and think they provide) and what families feel they actually receive (Holden and Lewine, 1982; Hatfield, 1983). The first step in bridging this gap (sometimes characterized by families as a "chasm") is to bring staff and family members together in a forum or activity which fosters mutual empathy. Depending upon the level of experience, knowledge, and sensitivity with which staff members begin, and depending upon financial and time constraints, this initial training (or sensitivity-enhancing) experience can range from a few hours to a full day or more. It would include some combination of the following activities:

1) A role-play presentation of a family-clinician interview. This can be done by a local "Mental Health Players" group if one exists or by staff and family member volunteers who have developed a script and rehearsed a bit. In any case, it should include multiple examples of how not to behave (often family members can role play experiences that have actually happened to them) in order to elicit audience reaction. A question-and-answer period in which the players stay in role during the dialogue with the audience invariably provides a stimulating conclusion. This activity is a good icebreaker and belongs near the beginning of a program.

2) An "expert" speaker. As psychoeducational programs for families are gaining wider acceptance, there is a growing pool of clinicians experienced in this area. Invite a speaker whose written work is familiar to some of the staff or one who has started a family program in a similar setting.

3) A panel of family members. It is virtually impossible to listen to the story of a person who has a chronically mentally ill child, parent, or sibling and remain unmoved. Likewise, when family members tell about their experiences with professionals, the clinicians in the au-

dience are more receptive since these are not their clients and they need not feel defensive or pushed to fix matters. Generally, the local NAMI chapter will recruit speakers for the panel at no cost, since one of their goals is to heighten professional sensitivity to family needs.

4) A panel of or a debate among professionals. A discussion of controversial issues in family work (for example, the effect of confidentiality requirements, attending to process versus content, education versus therapy) can highlight both theoretical and methodological points of interest. Hopefully, this will provide a reexamination by each clinician of his or her own biases.

5) Small group discussions. When a family member and a clinician co-lead a small (six-to-ten-person) discussion group composed of both family members and professionals, much can be learned. In a day-long workshop in Rockland County, New York ("Bridging the Gap," December, 1983), these groups met in the morning to explore what behaviors were unhelpful or unsupportive from each participant's perspective, and again in the afternoon to discuss beneficial and strengthening experiences. Leaders should be trained to model forthright but nonconfrontive communication and to keep the group process positive and productive. Participants have rated these experiences as quite beneficial.

6) Objective-setting. Too often training conferences have only a short-term effect due to a lack of direction-setting and follow-up. One valuable activity, best if saved until near the end of the session, is to develop a list of objectives which will result in some permanent changes in the agency's program. For example, here are some specific objectives that could be set at such meetings: planning additional training or supervision experiences; naming a task force whose mission is to create a family education seminar of specified length; setting a date for chart audit looking at the extent to which family service appears in the treatment plan. Each agency or insti-

tution will, of course, have its own goals, tailored to take advantage of its unique strengths and to rectify its identified deficiencies. Objectives which are specific, behavioral, and time-limited are most likely to be implemented. Administrators will want to set a definite time to follow up in order to see that objectives have been met.

While none of these activities is indispensable, nor is the list all-inclusive, it is imperative that family members be present as experts, as educators, as consultants. It is, after all, their plight that we wish to understand and ameliorate. Our past attempts to intuit their needs based on our own theoretical perspectives have been dismal failures; listening to what they tell us is sure to produce better results.

IDENTIFYING AND TRAINING STAFF

Once the agency is committed to increasing the availability and scope of educational, supportive services for families of the chronically mentally ill, the next step is to identify how and by whom these services will be provided. Rather than attempting to train all staff who might come into contact with families, it is probably preferable to select staff who have demonstrated a respectful attitude towards families and who are interested in expanding their expertise in this area. Psychiatrists' time is generally at great premium, and so they will probably participate less actively in family programs. However, it is important that family clinicians have the support and back-up of both medical and administrative personnel in order to function effectively.

Once staff are identified, deficiencies in their training or experience can be specified and rectified. For example, some may need training in behavioral techniques, while others will need to learn about the biochemistry and genetics of the psychoses. Some may benefit from case supervision at first, while others will need to interview patients with the goal of learning something about the phenomenology of mental illness. It is also important to set up channels of communication so that family clinicians can enhance their skills through mutual consultation and find out what they need to know from the patient's psychiatrist, primary therapist, ward or unit administrator, floor nurse, and other treatment staff. If this is done properly, family members will be saved the time and frustration of seeking out various staff members for different kinds of information. The family clinician will gather the information, clarify discrepancies, and interpret the findings to the family in a coherent manner. This is not to say that families should be cut off from other treatment personnel, although they may feel substantially less need to seek them out when family clinicians function optimally.

Which and how many staff members will be identified as family clinicians will depend on the particular setting. In some agencies, the case manager role may be feasibly expanded to encompass these duties. In rural outpatient setting, the community mental health nurse is the logical choice. In large inpatient settings, personnel from nursing, social work, psychology and psychiatry staff may be designated. Psychiatric hospitals may decide to pool resources, developing a core group of family clinicians who serve families from several different wards or units. Likewise, agencies may pool resources. For example, a transitional residence staff member and a day treatment staff member may team up to provide services to families of patients from both settings.

While clarity of roles is useful, rigidity is not. Other staff members can be incorporated into various aspects of the family education and support program as needed. For example, a psychiatrist may be invited to a family group meeting to discuss medications or a psychologist may be invited to give a mini-course on behavioral management techniques.

DEVELOPING A SUPPORT AND EDUCATIONAL PROGRAM

Services to families should be based on what families say they want and on what knowledge and skills professionals know families need when coping with a chronically mentally ill relative. Ideally, a range of services should be available, so that a particular program can be devised to suit an individual family member's needs. In the best of all possible worlds, a family support program would include at least the following components:

1) A time-limited educational group for all interested family members. This is particularly important for inpatient settings where patients may be newly diagnosed, but can also be offered in outpatient settings for families whose relatives have not been hospitalized and for those who did not receive adequate information (or were unable to absorb it) when their relative was hospitalized. Some agencies have found a full-day educational workshop tremendously valuable (Anderson, 1983), while others have held shorter evening sessions weekly over a period of four to 12 weeks, depending upon the material to be covered. In any case, the workshop should be held frequently enough that all families get a chance to participate before their relative leaves the agency or institution. For inpatient settings that have a short length of stay, this may mean having a brief (two-to-three-hour) offering which is repeated weekly or biweekly. In oupatient settings where patients will be followed for an extended period, it may be possible to offer a more extensive workshop three or four times a year.

At minimum, issues related to diagnosis, prognosis, treatment (particularly medication effects and side effects), discharge planning (for inpatient settings), and basic coping skills should be covered. It is also useful to provide an orientation to the agency or institution, including a description of programs, role and functions of various staff members and the range and availability of follow-up services. Finally, a representative from the local family support group (probably a National Alliance for the Mentally Ill affiliate) can be invited to introduce family members to the services available through NAMI.

We suggest providing as much information in writing as possible, since family members who are overwhelmed may find it difficult to retain all the information they want and need. A written program orientation, pamphlets about mental illness (many of which are available through the National Institute of Mental Health), brochures from NAMI, and reading lists (see Appendix A) are among the materials that family members will find valuable.

2) Weekly information "coffee hours." Particularly in inpatient, day hospital or sheltered living programs, families may derive great comfort and support from informal conversations with staff such as would be available at an evening coffee hour. The availability of staff on a regular basis decreases the sense of panic and being out of control that often plagues family members and reduces the number of phone calls to staff during the week. Staff members may rotate attendance, or one or more staff members may regularly host the activity with other staff dropping in from time to time. A short program may be offered at the meeting, but most of the time should be free for socializing, chatting about patients' progress, and sharing information or advice.

3) Time-limited skills-building workshops. If needs and interest warrant, various short-term programs in communication training, assertiveness, behavioral management, stress-management, and methods for coping with common problematic behaviors can be offered by staff with expertise in these areas. Again, joint sponsorship of such workshops by multiple agencies may be a parsimonious approach in terms of staff deployment. Local mental health associations and NAMI affiliates may also finance and sponsor such programs, drawing on expertise of local agency staff.

4) Ongoing family group counseling. This can be particularly valuable in outpatient, day program, and transitional residence settings in helping families cope with the chronic deficits and ongoing need for support and structure their relatives experience. While some part

of the group's time may be spent in learning from professionals various specific skills which can help reduce stress, an important component will be the empathy and sharing of ideas that family members offer each other. Reduction in feelings of isolation and enhancement of self-confidence in family members are common outcomes of such a program. In areas where the local family support group is active, professionals may choose to refer family members there, offering their own expertise on topics such as stress management, communication skills, and behavioral techniques to the group on an "as needed" basis rather than developing an in-house program of their own. This avoids duplication of service, runs less risk of covertly fostering "patienthood" in family members, and frees up staff time for other endeavors.

5) Ongoing individual family consultation and counseling. Some family members are not comfortable in group settings, while others need or prefer more intensive ongoing support. This may be particularly true for families who are relatively new to the system and who, therefore, have a lot to learn. Often these families feel the need to be in close contact with a clinician who is directly involved in their relative's care.

6) Special programs for children. Children with a mentally ill sibling or parent have special needs and concerns. They may feel guilty or fearful that they will get sick, too. They need information which is tailored to their cognitive capacities and relevant to their feelings. Adolescents may benefit from group discussions with their peers (similar to Alateen, perhaps), as well as from multiple family groups in which they and their parents meet together with others in similar situations along with professionals who can elicit their concerns, provide factual information, and encourage open communication about the illness within the family. Younger children may benefit from drawing, stories, puppets, and other play activities designed to enhance their

understanding of the illness and to assuage their fears. Parents of younger children will need guidance on how to help them understand and cope with the illness in their midst. The assessment of family needs can provide data regarding the number of children or adolescents who have relatives in treatment so that programs tailored to their needs can be implemented.

PROGRAM EVALUATION

Not all families will participate in all segments of the family program, nor will all agencies have all segments available. Some are more appropriate and feasible for certain kinds of settings than for others. Ideally, the system of mental health services for a particular city or region would provide access to a full range of family-oriented services through a cooperative arrangement. In addition, the services we suggest are by no means all inclusive. They are limited by our own experience and creativity. Agencies and families may jointly develop a larger or different list based on their evaluation of their own population and staff availability.

In any case, the program should build in an evaluation component to ensure that what is being provided is, in fact, what families want, and to allow for ongoing flexibility of programming. An advisory committee composed of family members and clinicians might be charged with this task, or participant feedback might be used to guide future planning. No matter how it is accomplished, we underline the need for built-in feedback, since in the past families have been subjected to all sorts of treatment by mental health professionals, treatment that families often found worthless or even harmful.

ISSUES IN GRADUATE EDUCATION AND TRAINING

To help the next generation of mental health clinicians respond more adequately to the needs of families of the mentally ill, certain changes in graduate curricula are in order. This section is addressed to administrators and educators who are in a position to institute these changes. First, course syllabi and reading lists need to be modified. Particularly for non-medical trainees, a thorough review of the considerable evidence pointing to genetic and biochemical factors in the etiology of psychosis should replace, or at least be included along with, the case-study-supported "family as specific causal agent" model, which at this time is mainly of historical interest. Though outdated and poorly supported by empirical evidence, it is still taught in most graduate programs. Students should, at the very least, be exposed to reviews which point out the methodological flaws and illogical reasoning which are inherent in this approach (Liem, 1980). They can also be exposed to surveys of families' needs (Hatfield, 1978; Holden and Lewine, 1982), as well as to alternative approaches by professionals which have recently gained considerable acceptance (e.g., McFarlane, 1983; Bernheim, 1982). Finally, students can become familiar with the growing educational literature written for family members (see Appendix A), so that they can refer families to these resources when appropriate.

In addition, families themselves can be a valuable resource in the training of future mental health professionals. Not only could they offer a valuable perspective on curriculum development committees, but they could be invited to speak at graduate seminars, grand rounds, panel discussions and other educational activities. In locations where the NAMI chapter meetings are open to professionals, trainees would gain a great deal of understanding by attending several meetings.

An intriguing notion, which would require cooperative training efforts across a geographical region, involves assigning trainees to patients rather than to agencies (Lewine, 1983). This would give the student a taste of what families go through and how the system works for (or against) them.

Just as courses and practicum experiences in counseling or psychotherapy technique are offered, so should courses on teaching technique, since much of what families request is education. Observation of professionals in didactic roles can be followed by supervised practice. Trainees will need to know what aspects of psychopathology and treatment to teach, how to translate professional jargon into lay language, how to use visual aids effectively in teaching families, and how to provide training in communication skills, behavioral management skills, and other pragmatic techniques.

Even though many trainees may ultimately find themselves in outpatient settings, working primarily with nonpsychotic clients, we feel this training will be of great benefit nonetheless. We are struck by how many community mental health clients have chronically mentally ill parents, siblings, or children and how often these clients have unresolved emotional issues with respect to the illness in the family. Ignorance, guilt, fear for one's own sanity, anger at the ill person or other family members, ongoing grief, and questions about how best to interact with the ill relative all emerge as treatment issues. Thus, the development of the attitude and skills we have discussed is applicable to all mental health professionals, regardless of the setting.

PROFESSIONAL REWARDS

We have come to see families as partners rather than as adversaries in the rehabilitation effort. We have learned to ask family members what they wanted from us, rather than providing what we thought they needed. We have developed the view that families are entitled to services for their own sake, not just as adjunct in the treatment of their ill relative. And we have discovered that working with families in this way can be tremendously gratifying. Not only do we have good reason to be hopeful that these interventions will have a positive impact on the patient's symptoms and capacity to remain in the community, but we can see that families feel, often for the first time, that their own needs are being met. We watch them develop confidence in their own skills at managing the illness and we see that they begin to take pleasure in daily activities again. We also notice that when our work with chronic patients becomes burdensome and we begin to feel helpless and hopeless, it is the family work that gratifies our need to be helpful, to make a positive difference in somebody's life. While ultimately cure and prevention of chronic mental illness lie in the hands of biochemical researchers, we have found that, in partnership with loving, concerned family members, we are able to reduce somewhat the suffering of those presently afflicted.

APPENDICES

A

EDUCATIONAL RESOURCES
FOR FAMILIES

The following list is not all-inclusive. Rather, it represents a start-
ing point for exploring materials of potential value to families. It
includes only books. A more extensive listing, compiled by family
members themselves, is available from the National Alliance for the
Mentally Ill, 1901 North Fort Myer Drive, Suite 500, Arlington, VA
22209.

GENERAL

Andreason, N. C. (1974). *Understanding mental illness, a layman's
guide.* Minneapolis: Augsburg Publishing House.
Bernheim, K. F., Lewine, R. R. J., & Beale, C. T. (1982). *The caring
family: Living with chronic mental illness.* New York: Random
House.
Hatfield, A. B. (1984). *Coping with mental illness in the family: The
family guide.* Baltimore: University of Maryland.
Korpell, H. S. (1984). *How you can help: A guide for families of psy-
chiatric hospital patients.* Washington: American Psychiatric
Press.
Morrison, J. R. (1981). *Your brother's keeper: A guide for families
confronting psychiatric illness.* Chicago: Nelson-Hall.
Park, C. C. & Shapiro, L. N. (1976). *You are not alone.* Boston: Lit-
tle, Brown.
Sheehan, S. (1982). *Is there no place on earth for me?* New York: Ran-
dom House.
Snyder, S. H. (1980). *Biological aspects of mental disorders.* New
York: Oxford University Press.
Snyder, S. H. (1975). *Madness and the brain.* New York: McGraw-
Hill.
Vine, P. (1982). *Families in pain: Children, siblings, spouses, and*

parents of the mentally ill speak out. New York: Pantheon Press.

SCHIZOPHRENIA

Bernheim, K. F., & Lewine, R. R. J. (1979). *Schizophrenia: Symptoms, causes and treatments.* New York: W. W. Norton & Company.

Gottesman, I. I., & Shields, J. (1982). *Schizophrenia: The epigenetic puzzle.* New York: Cambridge University Press.

O'Brien, P. (1978). *The disordered mind: What we now know about schizophrenia.* Englewood Cliffs, NJ: Prentice-Hall.

Rollin, H. (Ed.). (1980). *Coping with schizophrenia.* London: Burnett Books.

Seeman, S. E., Littmann, S. K., Plummer, E., & Thornton, J. F. (1982). *Living and working with schizophrenia: Information and support for patients and their families, friends, employers, and teachers.* Toronto: University of Toronto Press.

Torrey, E. F. (1983). *Surviving schizophrenia, a family manual.* New York: Harper and Row.

Tsuang, M. T. (1982). *Schizophrenia: The facts.* New York: Oxford University Press.

Walsh, M. (1985). *Schizophrenia: Straight talk for family and friends.* New York: Morrow.

Wasow, M. (1982). *Coping with schizophrenia: A survival manual for parents, relatives, and friends.* Palo Alto, CA: Science & Behavior Books.

Wing, J. K. (1978). *Schizophrenia: Towards a new synthesis.* New York: Academic Press.

AFFECTIVE DISORDER

Cammer, L. (1968). *Up from depression.* New York: Simon & Schuster.

Fieve, R. (1975). *Mood swings: The third revolution in psychiatry.* New York: Morrow.

Greist, J. H., & Jefferson, J. W. (1984). *Depression and its treatment: Help for the nation's #1 mental problem.* Washington: American Psychiatric Press.

Kline, N. S. (1974). *From sad to glad.* New York: Ballantine Books.

Sturgeon, W. (1979). *Depression, how to recognize it, how to treat it, and how to grow from it.* Englewood Cliffs, NJ: Prentice-Hall.

SOCIAL ISSUES

Des Jardins, C. (1980). *How to organize an effective parent/advocacy group and move bureaucracies.* Chicago: Coordinating Council for Handicapped Children.

Ennis, B. J., & Emery, R. D. (1978). *The rights of mental patients: An American Civil Liberties Union handbook.* New York: Avon Books.

Krauss, J. B., & Slavinsky, A. T. (1982). *The chronically ill psychiatric patient and the community.* Boston: Boston Blackwell Scientific Publications.

Moore, R. J., Morton, K., Barr, A. S., & Abell, S. (1979). *Estate planning for families with handicapped dependents.* Baltimore: Maryland Institute for Continuing Professional Education of Lawyers.

Stein, L. I. (1979). *Community support systems for the long-term patient.* San Francisco: Jossey-Bass.

Talbott, J. A. (1978). *The chronic mental patient: Problems, solutions, and recommendations for a public policy.* Washington: American Psychiatric Association.

B

AFFILIATES OF THE NATIONAL ALLIANCE FOR THE MENTALLY ILL

The national office of NAMI is at 1901 North Fort Myer Drive, Suite 500, Arlington, VA 22209 (703-524-7600). In states with statewide organizations, smaller local affiliates are not listed.

ALABAMA

Jefferson-Blount St. Clair M.H./
  M.R. Authority
3820 Third Avenue, South,
  Suite 100
Birmingham, AL 35222
(205) 595-4555

Huntsville Support Alliance for
  the Mentally Ill
403 Westburg Avenue
Huntsville, AL 35801
(205) 882-2162

Mobile Family Support Group
4508 Kingsway Ct.
Mobile, AL 36608

ALASKA

REACH
c/o Alaska Mental Health
  Association
2611 Fairbanks St.
Anchorage, AK 99503
(907) 276-1705

Fairbanks AMI
P.O. Box 2543
Fairbanks, AK 99707
(907) 452-3733

Juneau AMI
Box 211247
Auke Bay, AK 99821

Kenai AMI
P.O. Box 301
Soldotna, AK 99669

ARIZONA

Arizona Alliance for the Mentally Ill
4109 E. Catalina
Phoenix, AZ 85018
(602) 296-1221

ARKANSAS

Help and Hope, Inc.
Arkansas Families and Friends
of the Mentally Ill
4313 W. Markham Hendrix
Hall 125
Little Rock, AR 72201
(501) 661-1548

CALIFORNIA

California Alliance for the
Mentally Ill
1818 H. Street, #6
Sacramento, CA 95814
(916) 443-6417

COLORADO

Colorado Alliance for the Mentally Ill
P.O. Box 28008
Lakewood, CO 80228
(303) 321-3104

CONNECTICUT

Connecticut Alliance for the
Mentally Ill
284 Battis Road
Hamden, CT 06514
(203) 248-3351

DISTRICT OF COLUMBIA

Threshold – D.C.
2200 South Dakota Avenue,
N.E.
Washington, D.C. 20018
(202) 636-4239

FLORIDA

Manatee Mental Health Center
Family Support Group
115 Manatee Avenue W.
Bradenton, FL 33505

AMI of Brevard County
2718 Hillcrest Avenue
Titusville, FL 32796
(305) 267-8942

Broward Advocates for the
Mentally Ill
16771 Harbor Court
Fort Lauderdale, FL 33326
(305) 389-1657

REACH
660 9th Street N. Suite 37
Naples, FL 33940
(813) 261-5405

REACH
P.O. Box 06137
Ft. Myers, FL 33906
(813) 334-3537

Family Support Group
11331 Ponce de Leon Blvd.
Brooksville, FL 33512
(904) 799-4094

Martin & St. Lucie County
AMI
Box #2178
Stuart, FL 33495-2178
(305) 335-7293

Community Advocates for the
 Mentally Ill
c/o Fellowship House
5711 S. Dixie Hwy.
Miami, FL 33143
(305) 271-7749

REACH
660 9th Street, N., Suite 37
Naples, FL 33940

AMI of North Central Florida
402 S.W. 41st Street
Gainesville, FL 32607
(904) 376-2710

LOMI
MHA of Bay Co.
P.O. Box 2245
1316 Harrison Avenue, Suite
 203
Panama City, FL 32401

Alliance for the Mentally Ill
 of Palm Beach
666 Laconia Cir.
Lake Worth, FL 33463
(305) 968-6543

Concerned Relatives and
 Friends of South Florida
 State Hospital, Inc.
9109 N.W. 81st Ct.
Tamarac, FL 33321

Families Together for Mental
 Health
1355 Cambridge Dr.
Venice, FL 33595
(813) 484-1484

GEORGIA

Georgia Friends of the Mentally Ill
1390 DeClair Drive
Atlanta, GA 30329
(404) 636-1840

HAWAII

Hawaii Families and Friends
 of Schizophrenics, Inc.
P.O. Box 10532
Honolulu, HI 96816
(808) 487-5456

IDAHO

Idaho Alliance for the Mentally Ill
321 Buchanan
American Falls, ID 83211
(208) 226-2346

ILLINOIS

AMI Illinois State Coalition
P.O. Box 2363
Glenview, IL 60025
(312) 441-2131

INDIANA

Ft. Wayne AMI
P.O. Box 8186
Ft. Wayne, IN 46808
(219) 432-4085

Marion County TLC
555 Sunset Blvd.
Greenwood, IN 46142
(317) 881-3966

South Bend AMI
1140 E. Ewing
South Bend, IN 46613
(219) 289-1511

IOWA

Iowa Alliance for the Mentally
Ill
520 SE First St. (Box 334)
Eagle Grove, IA 50533
(515) 448-5036

KANSAS

Prairie View Community Support Program
Box 467
Newton, KS 67114
(316) 283-2400

Families for Mental Health, Inc.
P.O. Box 2452
Shawnee Mission, KS 66201
(913) 432-8240

Families for Mental Health
Shawnee Co.
4538 NE Meriden Rd.
Topeka, KS 66617
(913) 286-1882

Wyandotte County Families
for Mental Health
36th at Eaton
Kansas City, KS 66103

KENTUCKY

Ashland Area AMI
1636 Stewart Lane
Ashland, KY 41101

Schizophrenia Association of
Louisville
7702 Brownwood Dr.
Louisville, KY 40218
(502) 491-1542

LOUISIANA

Family Support for Mental
Health
1633 Letitia Street
Baton Rouge, LA 70808

Friends Alliance for the Mentally Ill
6028 Magazine St.
New Orleans, LA 70118
(504) 895-2891

Families and Friends for Mental Health
178 Ronald Blvd.
Lafayette, LA 70503
(318) 232-1808

New Hope for Mental Health
c/o Barbara Yerkey
Route 13, Box 156
Lake Charles, LA 70611
(318) 436-6879

Family Support Group
500 Walnut St.
New Orleans, LA 70118

Caddo-Bossier AMI
159 Bruce Street
Shreveport, LA 71105
(318) 861-7469

Association for Research in
Children's Emotional Disorders
P.O. Box 511
Westwego, LA 70094

MAINE

Maine State AMI, Inc.
P.O. Box 370
Oakland, ME 04963
(207) 547-3639

MARYLAND

AMI of Maryland, Inc.
P.O. Box 336
Kensington, MD 20895
(301) 229-0928

MASSACHUSETTS

AMI of Massachusetts, Inc.
227 Mt. Hope Road
Somerset, MA 02726
(617) 678-9664

MICHIGAN

AMI of Michigan
P.O. Box 515
Mirmingham, MI 48012
(313) 855-9820

MINNESOTA

Mental Health Advocates Coalition of Minnesota, Inc.
265 Ft. Rd. (W. 7th St.)
St. Paul, MN 55102
(612) 222-2741

MISSISSIPPI

Families and Friends of the
Mentally Ill
P.O. Box 1286
Hattiesburg, MS 39401
(601) 583-0948

MISSOURI

Missouri AMI
135 W. Adams, Room G-9
St. Louis, MO 63122
(314) 966-4670

MONTANA

Great Falls AMI
North Central Montana MHC
P.O. Box 3048
Great Falls, MT 59403

FLAME
640 Conrad Drive
Kalispell, MT 59901

Helena AMI
479 S. Park
Helena, MT 59601
(406) 443-6096

A New Beginning for the
Mentally Disordered
2405 39th Street
Missoula, MT 59807
(406) 251-2146

Genesis House Inc
P.O. Box 350
Stevensville, MT 59870

NEBRASKA

AMI of Nebraska, Inc.
Lincoln Center Bldg.
215 Centennial Mall South
Lincoln, NE 68508
(402) 467-6285

NEVADA

Nevada Alliance for the Mentally Ill
3229 Anacapa
Las Vegas, NV 89102
(702) 873-1297

NEW HAMPSHIRE

NAMI in New Hampshire
P.O. Box 544
Peterborough, NH 03458
(603) 924-3069

NEW JERSEY

Atlantic Co. MH Family Support Group
c/o CCP
1125 Pacific Ave.
Atlantic City, NJ 08401
(609) 344-8335

Family Organization of the
Mid-Bergen Community MHC
11 Park Pl
Paramus, NJ 07652
(201) 265-8200

M.H. Advocacy Group
340 12th St.
Palisades Park, NJ 07650
(201) 947-1470

Focus Mental Health – Delaware
House
Wood and Pearl Sts.
Burlington, NJ 08016

FACE
P.O. Box 1322
Delran, NJ 08075
(609) 877-2168

Pioneers for Mental Health
19 E. Ormond Ave.
Cherry Hill, NJ 08034
(609) 428-1300

Concerned Families for
Improved Mental Health
Services
424 Main St.
E. Orange, NJ 07018
(201) 677-1540

Concerned Citizens for Chronic
Psychiatric Adults
521 Hayward Street
Bound Brook, NJ 08805
(201) 356-2308

Concerned Families of the
Mentally Ill
c/o Frank J. Marolt
170 Center Avenue
Chatham, NJ 07928

West Bergen MHC
74 Oak Street
Ridgewood, NJ 07450

TLC of Salem Co.
R.D. 2, Box 346
Woodstown, NJ 08098
(609) 678-7846

Family and Friends of the
Mentally Ill
200 S. Feltus St., #35
So. Amboy, NJ 08879

NEW MEXICO

State Alliance for Mental Illness, New Mexico
819 Bishops Lodge Road
Sante Fe, NM 87501
(505) 983-2584

NEW YORK

AMI of New York State
42 Elting Avenue
New Paltz, NY 12561
(914) 255-5134

NORTH CAROLINA

North Carolina Alliance for
the Mentally Ill
P.O. Box 10557
Greensboro, NC 27404
(919) 275-7127

NORTH DAKOTA

REACH
1113 10 Street N.W.
Minot, ND 58701

OHIO

Ohio Family Coalition for the
Mentally Ill
199 S. Central Ave.
Columbus, OH 43223
(614) 274-7000

OKLAHOMA

REACH
5104 N. Francis, Suite B
Oklahoma City, OH 73118
(405) 524-6363

Families in Touch
MHA in Tulsa
5 W. 22nd St.
Tulsa, OK 74114
(918) 599-9403

OREGON

Oregon Alliance for Advocates
of the Mentally Ill
P.O. Box 47
Thurston, OR 97482

PENNSYLVANIA

Pennsylvania AMI
840 Grand View Blvd.
Lancaster, PA 17601

RHODE ISLAND

East Bay Advocates
19 Barney Street
Warren, RI 02885
(401) 245-2386

Kent County Mental Health
Family Support Group
116 Long Street
Warwick, RI 02886

Families & Advocates for the
Mentally Ill of Newport Co.
P.O. Box 837
Newport, RI 02840

MHA Project Reach Out
89 Park St.
Providence, RI 02908

SOUTH CAROLINA

Families and Friends of the
Mentally Ill
P.O. Box 32084
Charleston, SC 29417
(803) 795-4600

Mid-Carolina FFMI
P.O. Box 61075
Columbia, SC 29260
(803) 766-2327

Piedmont Family and Friends
of the Mentally Ill
112 Robin Street
Clemson, SC 29631
(803) 654-1189

SOUTH DAKOTA

Northeastern MHC Family
Support Group
Box 550
Aberdeen, SD 57401
(605) 225-1010

Brookings Area MHA
Box 273
Brookings, SD 57006
(605) 692-5673

TENNESSEE

Mental Health Association of
Hamilton County
Families in Touch
921 East Third Street
Chattanooga, TN 37403

Families in Touch
c/o Mental Health Association
of Knox County
6712 Kingston Pike
Knoxville, TN 37919

AMI of Memphis
P.O. Box 17304
Memphis, TN 38187-0304
(901) 276-0239

Families in Touch
c/o MHA in Nashville
250 Venture Cir., #204
Nashville, TN 37228
(615) 242-6487

TEXAS

Texas AMI
5009 Rain Creek Parkway
Austin, TX 78759
(512) 346-0872

UTAH

Utah AMI
P.O. Box 26561
Salt Lake City, UT 84126
(801) 484-3314

VERMONT

AMI Vermont
9 Andrews Avenue
So. Burlington, VT 05401

VIRGINIA

We Care
1245 Chatham Road
Waynesboro, VA 11980
(703) 942-4043

Blue Ridge Family Alliance
for the Mentally Ill
1602 Gordon Avenue
Charlottesville, VA 22903

Southside Affiliate – Town
House Friends
127 North St.
Farmville, VA 23901
(804) 392-8307

Rappahannock AMI
c/o Joyce Haddock
Route 1, Box 1800
Partlow, VA 22534

Massanutten Family Support
Group
276 W. Market St.
Harrisonburg, VA 22801
(703) 433-1593

Norfolk Community Services
Board
201 Granby Mall, Suite 103
Norfolk, VA 23510

Pathways to Independence
P.O. Box 651
McLean, VA 22101
(703) 671-9619

Northwestern VA Family Support Group for the Mentally Ill
315 Wood Avenue
Winchester, VA 22601
(703) 662-5504

Richmond Area Schizophrenia Foundation
4010 W. Franklin St.
Richmond, VA 23221
(804) 358-6980

Schizophrenia Foundation of VA
Box 2342
Virginia Beach, VA 23450
(804) 499-2041

WASHINGTON

Washington State Coalition of Family Associations
906 E. Shelby
Seattle, WA 98102
(206) 322-0408

WEST VIRGINIA

Charleston AMI
5453 Kingswood Lane
Charleston, WV 25313

AMI of Eastern Panhandle
404 Edgemont Terrace
Martinsburg, WV 25401
(304) 263-9847

WISCONSIN

AMI of Wisconsin, Inc.
Rt. 8, 1997 HWY PB
Verona, WI 53593
(608) 845-6141

WYOMING

Family Alliance for the Mentally Ill
845 South Grant Street
Casper, WY 82601
(307) 234-6246

CANADA

Association of Relatives & Friends of the Mentally and Emotionally Ill
P.O. Box 322, Snowdon Branch
Montreal, Quebec H3X 3T6
(514) 937-5351

VIRGIN ISLANDS

St. Croix Concerned Citizens for Mental Health, Inc.
P.O. Box 937 Kings Hill
St. Croix, VI 00850

REFERENCES

Adams-Greenly, M., & Moynihan, R. T. (1983). Helping children of fatally ill parents. *American Journal of Orthopsychiatry, 53,* 219–229.

Ahlfield, J. E., Soler, N. G., & Marcus, S. D. (1983). Adolescent diabetes mellitus: Parent/child perspectives of the effect of the disease on family and social interactions. *Diabetes Care, 6,* 393–398.

Albee, G. (1981). Remarks made at a conference: An ounce of prevention: Reorienting mental health priorities. *Self-Help Reporter, 5,* 1–2.

Anderson, C. M. (1983). A psychoeducational program for families of patients with schizophrenia. In W. R. McFarlane (Ed.), *Family therapy in schizophrenia* (pp. 99–116). New York: Guilford.

Anderson, C. M., Hogarty, G. E., & Reiss, D. J. (1980). The family treatment of adult schizophrenic patients: A psychoeducational approach. *Schizophrenia Bulletin, 6,* 490–505.

Anderson, C. M., Hogarty, G. E., & Reiss, D. J. (1981). The psychoeducational family treatment of schizophrenia. In M. J. Goldstein (Ed.), *New developments in interventions with families of schizophrenics* (pp. 79–94). San Francisco: Jossey-Bass.

Andreasen, N. (1984). *The broken brain.* New York: Harper and Row.

Ayd, F. J. (1961). A survey of drug-induced extrapyramidal reactions. *Journal of the American Medical Association, 175,* 1054–1060.

Bachrach, L. L. (1976). *Deinstitutionalization: An analytical review and sociological perspective.* Department of Health, Education and Welfare, Publication No. (ADM) 76-351.

Bachrach, L. L. (1980). Overview: Model programs for chronic mental patients. *American Journal of Psychiatry, 137,* 1023–1031.

Beale, C. T. (1982). *Chronic mental illness: The family's response.* Unpublished manuscript.

Beers, C. W. (1960). *A mind that found itself* (5th ed., originally published, 1908). Garden City: Doubleday.

Bellack, A. S. (Ed.). (1984). *Schizophrenia: Treatment, management and rehabilitation.* Orlando: Grune and Stratton.

Berkowitz, R., Kuipers, L., Eberlein-Frief, R., & Leff, J. (1981). Lowering expressed emotion in relatives of schizophrenics. In M. J. Goldstein (Ed.), *New developments in interventions with families of schizophrenics* (pp. 27-48). San Francisco: Jossey-Bass.

Bernheim, K. F. (1982). Supportive family counseling. *Schizophrenia Bulletin, 8,* 634-641.

Bernheim, K. F., & Lewine, R. R. J. (1979). *Schizophrenia: Symptoms, causes, treatments.* New York: W. W. Norton & Company.

Bernheim, K. F., Lewine, R. R. J., & Beale, C. T. (1982). *The caring family: Living with chronic mental illness.* New York: Random House.

Borghi, J. H. (1968). Premature psychotherapy and the patient-therapist relationship. *American Journal of Psychotherapy, 22,* 460-473.

Borus, J. F. (1981). Deinstitutionalization of the chronically mentally ill. *New England Journal of Medicine, 305,* 339-342.

Brody, E. M. (1985). Parent care as a normative family stress. *Gerontologist, 25,* 19-29.

"Bridging the Gap" Conference, Dec '83. (1984). *FOCUS: The Journal of the Rockland County Mental Health Association, Inc.,* 3-34.

Brown, G. W. (1959). Experiences of discharged chronic schizophrenic mental hospital patients in various types of living group. *Milbank Memorial Fund Quarterly, 37,* 105-131.

Brown, G. W., Birley, J. L. T., & Wing, J. K. (1972). Influence of family life on the course of schizophrenic disorder: A replication. *British Journal of Psychiatry, 121,* 241-258.

Brown, G., Carstairs, G. M., & Topping, G. (1958). Post-hospital adjustment of chronic mental patients. *Lancet, 2,* 685-689.

Cantor, M. J. (1983). Strain among caregivers: A study of experience in the United States. *Gerontologist, 23,* 597-604.

Caton, C. L. M. (1984). *Management of chronic schizophrenia.* New York, Oxford University Press.

Clark, N. M., & Rakowski, W. (1983). Family caregivers of older adults: Improving helping skills. *Gerontologist, 23,* 637-642.

Creer, C., & Wing, J. K. (1975). Living with a schizophrenic patient. *British Journal of Hospital Medicine,* 73-82.

Creer, C., & Wing, J. K. (1974). *Schizophrenia at home.* London: Institute of Psychiatry.

Doherty, E. G. (1975). Labeling effects in psychiatric hospitalization. *Archives of General Psychiatry, 32,* 562-568.

Doll, W. (1976). Family coping with the mentally ill: An unanticipated problem of deinstitutionalization. *Hospital and Community Psychiatry, 27,* 183–185.

Endicott, J., Herz, M. I., & Gibbon, M. (1978). Brief versus standard hospitalization: the differential costs. *American Journal of Psychiatry, 135,* 707–712.

Erickson, K. T. (1962). Notes on the sociology of deviance. *Social Problems, 9,* 307–314.

Falloon, I. R. H., Boyd, J. L., & McGill, C. W. (1984). *Family care of schizophrenia.* New York: Guilford Press.

Falloon, I. R. H., Boyd, J. L., McGill, C. W., Razani, J., Moss, H. B., & Gilderman, A. M. (1982). Family management in the prevention of exacerbations of schizophrenia. *New England Journal of Medicine, 306,* 1437–1440.

Falloon, I. R. H., Boyd, J. L., McGill, C. W., Strong, J. S., & Moss, H. B. (1981). Family management training in the community care of schizophrenia. In M. J. Goldstein (Ed.), *New developments in interventions with families of schizophrenics* (pp. 61–77). San Francisco: Jossey-Bass.

Falloon, I. R. H., & Liberman, R. P. (1983). Behavioral family interventions in the management of chronic schizophrenia. In W. R. McFarlane (Ed.), *Family therapy in schizophrenia* (pp. 117–140). New York: Guilford.

Garatt, M. W. (1985). Disclosing diagnosis: A parent's view [Letter to the editor]. *Hospital and Community Psychiatry, 36,* 191.

Goffman, E. (1961). *Asylums.* Garden City: Anchor Books, Doubleday.

Goldberg, S. C., Schooler, N. R., Hogarty, G. E., & Roper, M. (1977). Prediction of relapse in schizophrenic outpatients treated by drug and social therapy. *Archives of General Psychiatry, 34,* 171 –184.

Goldman, H. H. (1982). Mental illness and family burden: A public health perspective. *Hospital and Community Psychiatry, 33,* 557–560.

Goldstein, M. J. (1984). Family intervention programs. In A. S. Bellack (Ed.), *Schizophrenia: Treatment, management and rehabilitation* (pp. 281–305). Orlando: Grune and Stratton.

Goldstein, M. J., & Doane, J. A. (1982). Family factors in the onset, course, and treatment of schizophrenic spectrum disorders. *Journal of Nervous and Mental Disease, 170,* 692–700.

Goldstein, M. J., & Kopeikin, H. S. (1981). Short-and long-term effects of combining drug and family therapy. In M. J. Goldstein (Ed.), *New developments in interventions with families of schizophrenics* (pp. 5–26). San Francisco: Jossey-Bass.

Goldstein, M. J., & Rodnick, E. H. (1975). The family's contribution to the etiology of schizophrenia: Current status. *Schizophrenia Bulletin, 14,* 48–63.

Grad, J., & Sainsbury, P. (1968). The effects that patients have on their families in a community care and a control psychiatric service – a two-year follow-up. *British Journal of Psychiatry, 114,* 265–278.

Green, R. S. (1984). Why schizophrenic patients should be told their diagnosis. *Hospital and Community Psychiatry, 35,* 76–77.

Greenblatt, M. (1977). Psychiatry and the third revolution. *Psychiatric Annals, 7,* 7–9, 24–29.

Grunebaum, H. (1984). Comments on Terkelsen's "Schizophrenia and the family: II. Adverse effects of family therapy." *Family Process, 23,* 421–428.

Gunderson, J. G., & Elliott, G. R. (1985). The interface between borderline personality disorder and affective disorder. *American Journal of Psychiatry, 142,* 277–299.

Haley, W. E. (1983). A family-behavioral approach to the treatment of the cognitively impaired elderly. *Gerontologist, 23,* 18–20.

Harding, C., Zubin, J., & Strauss, J. (in press). Chronicity in schizophrenia: Fact, partial fact, or artifact? *Hospital and Community Psychiatry.*

Hatfield, A. B. (1978). Psychological costs of schizophrenia to the family. *Social Work,* Sept., 355–359.

Hatfield, A. B. (1979). Help-seeking behavior in families of schizophrenics. *American Journal of Community Psychology, 7,* 563–569.

Hatfield, A. B. (1983). What families want of family therapists. In W. R. McFarlane (Ed.), *Family therapy in schizophrenia* (pp. 41–65). New York: Guilford.

Hatfield, B. A. (July 1984a). Coping with a mentally ill family member. Presented at National Alliance for the Mentally Ill Conference, Los Angeles.

Hatfield, A. B. (1984b). The family. In J. A. Talbott (Ed.), *The chronic mental patient: Five years later* (pp. 307–323). New York: Grune and Stratton.

Heine, R., & Grosman, H. (1960). Initial expectations of the doctor-patient interaction as a factor in the continuance in psychotherapy. *Psychiatry, 23,* 275–278.

Heinrichs, D. W., & Carpenter, W. T. (1983). The coordination of family therapy with other treatment modalities for schizophrenia. In W. R. McFarlane (Ed.), *Family therapy in schizophrenia* (pp. 267–287). New York: Guilford.

Henn, F. A., & Nasrallah, H. A. (1982). *Schizophrenia as a brain disease.* New York: Oxford University Press.

Herz, M. I., Endicott, J., & Gibbon, M. (1979). Brief hospitalization. *Archives of General Psychiatry, 36,* 701–705.

Herz, M. I., & Melville, C. (1980). Relapse in schizophrenia. *American Journal of Psychiatry, 137,* 801-805.

Holden, D. F., & Lewine, R. R. J. (1982). How families evaluate mental health professionals, resources, and effects of illness. *Schizophrenia Bulletin, 8,* 628-633.

Kondziela, J. R. (1984). Disclosing diagnosis [letter to the editor] and reply of R. S. Green. *Hospital and Community Psychiatry, 35,* 621.

Kopeikin, H. S., Marshall, V., & Goldstein, M. J. (1983). Stages and impact of crisis-oriented family therapy in the aftercare of acute schizophrenia. In W. R. McFarlane (Ed.), *Family therapy in schizophrenia* (pp. 69-98). New York: Guilford.

Kreisman, D., Simmons, S., & Joy, V. (1979). *Deinstitutionalization and the family's wellbeing,* New York: New York State Psychiatric Institute.

Kundler, H. S. (1984). Disclosing diagnosis, continued [letter to the editor] and reply of R. S. Green. *Hospital and Community Psychiatry, 35,* 731-732.

Lamb, H. R. (1981). What did we really expect from deinstitutionalization? *Hospital and Community Psychiatry, 32,* 105-109.

Leff, J., Kuipers, L., Berkowitz, R., Eberlein-Vries, R., & Sturgeon, D. (1982). A controlled trial of social intervention in the families of schizophrenic patients. *British Journal of Psychiatry, 141,* 121-134.

Lewine, R. R. J. (1983). Parents: Mental health professionals' scapegoats. In E. Sigel & L. M. Laosa (Eds.), *Changing families* (pp. 925-933). New York: Plenum Press.

Liem, J. H. (1980). Family studies of schizophrenia: An update and commentary. *Schizophrenia Bulletin, 6,* 429-455.

MacDonald, N. (1960). Living with schizophrenia. *Canadian Medical Association Journal, 82,* 218-221, 678-681.

McFarlane, W. R. (Ed.). (1983). *Family therapy in schizophrenia.* New York: Guilford.

McFarlane, W. R., & Terkelsen, K. G. (April 1985). Living with schizophrenia. Presented at American Orthopsychiatric Association, New York.

Meehl, R. (1962). Schizotaxia, schizotypy, schizophrenia. *American Psychologist, 17,* 827-838.

Meltzer, H., & Stahl, S. (1976). The dopamine hypothesis of schizophrenia: A review. *Schizophrenia Bulletin, 2,* 19-76.

NIMH. (1984). *Protocol for treatment strategies in schizophrenia.*

Ozarin, L. D., & Sharfstein, S. S. (1978). The aftermaths of deinstitutionalization: Problems and solutions. *Psychiatric Quarterly, 50,* 128-132.

Paykel, E. S. (Ed.). (1982). *Handbook of affective disorders.* New York: Guilford Press.

Pinkston, E. M., & Linsk, N. L. (1984). Behavioral family intervention with the impaired elderly. *Gerontologist, 24,* 576-583.

Rachlin, S. (1978). When schizophrenia comes marching home. *Psychiatric Quarterly, 50,* 202-210.

Reynolds, I., & Hoult, J. E. (1984). The relatives of the mentally ill. *Journal of Nervous and Mental Disease, 172,* 480-489.

Rothman, D. J. (1971). *The discovery of the asylum, social order and disorder in the new republic.* Boston: Little, Brown.

Ryglewicz, H. (1983). How can professionals help families and patients? *The Information Exchange on Young Adult Chronic Patients, 2,* 6.

Scherl, D. J., & Macht, L. B. (1979). Deinstitutionalization in the absence of consensus. *Hospital and Community Psychiatry, 30,* 599-604.

Snyder, K. S., & Liberman, R. P. (1981). Family assessment and intervention with schizophrenics at risk for relapse. In M. J. Goldstein (Ed.), *New developments in interventions with families of schizophrenics* (pp. 49-60). San Francisco: Jossey-Bass.

Stein, L. I., & Test, M. A. (1980). Alternative to mental hospital treatment. I. Conceptual model, treatment program, and clinical evaluation. *Archives of General Psychiatry, 37,* 392-397.

Talbott, J. A. (1978). *The death of the asylum.* New York: Grune & Stratton.

Terkelsen, K. G. (1983). Schizophrenia and the family: II. Adverse effects of family therapy. *Family Process, 22,* 191-200.

Terkelsen, K. G., & Cole, S. A. (1984). Methodological flaws in the schizophrenic hypothesis: Implications for psychiatric education. Unpublished manuscript.

Test, M. A., & Stein, L. I. (1980). Alternative to mental hospital treatment. III. Social cost. *Archives of General Psychiatry, 37,* 409-412.

Vaughn, C. E., & Leff, J. P. (1976). The influence of family and social factors on the course of psychiatric illness: A comparison of schizophrenic and depressed neurotic patients. *British Journal of Psychiatry, 129,* 125-137.

Vaughn, C. E., Snyder, K. S., Jones, S., Freeman, W. B., & Falloon, I. R. H. (1984). Family factors in schizophrenic relapse. *Archives of General Psychiatry, 41,* 1169-1177.

Vine, P. (1982). *Families in pain: Children, siblings, spouses and parents of the mentally ill speak out.* New York: Pantheon Press.

Wechsler, J. A. (1972). *In a darkness.* New York: W. W. Norton & Company.

Wilshaw, B., & Aplin, M. (1981). A terminal care and bereavement counseling service. *Health Visit, 54,* 333-336.

Wilson, L. (1968). *This stranger, my son: A mother's story.* New York: Putnam.

Wing, J. K. (1962). Institutionalism in mental hospitals. *British Journal of Social and Clinical Psychology, 1,* 38–51.
Wing, J. K., & Brown, G. W. (1970). *Institutionalism and schizophrenia.* London: Cambridge University Press.
Worden, J. W. (1982). *Grief counseling and grief therapy: A handbook for the mental health practitioner.* New York: Springer.
Yess, J. P. (1981). What families of the mentally ill want. *Community Support Service Journal, 2,* 1–3.
Zubin, J., & Spring, B. (1977). Vulnerability: A new view of schizophrenia. *Journal of Abnormal Psychology, 96,* 103–126.

INDEX

acronyms, professional, 162–63
addiction, fear of, 77–78
adolescent support programs, 210
advocacy, *see* family advocacy
affective disorders:
  interpersonal distance in, 27
  patient informed of diagnosis of,
    66–69
  see also expressed emotion;
    specific affective disorders
aggressive behavior, 118–23
  family's options and, 123–24
  immediate response to, 120
  outside help for, 124
  prevention of, 120–22
  purposeful, 122–23
  warning signals in, 119–20
Albee, George, 168–69
alcohol abuse, 81–82, 128–29
Anderson, C. M., 43, 44–46
anger, family's, 19, 52, 190–91
anxiety, family's, 20
assertiveness, family's, 194
asylums, *see* institutionalization

Beale, C. T., 25
Beers, Clifford, 5
behavior change strategies, family's,
    28–29, 109–40
  for aggression, 118–23
  for carelessness, 124–25
  communication skills in, 104–8
  contract used in, 90–92, 123,
    126–27
  for drug or alcohol abuse, 128–29
  experimental approach to, 58–59
  family meeting in, 92–93

for financial irresponsibility,
    129–31
for inappropriate sexual behav-
    ior, 136–39
for institutionalized behavior, 139
for noncompliance with treat-
    ment, 131–35
for panhandling, 135–36
for passivity, 110–15
for psychotic symptoms, 125–27
for social withdrawal, 110–15
for suicidal behavior, 115–18
Berkowitz, R., 40–41, 42
biases, therapist's:
  confidentiality issue and, 159, 189
  family's assessment of, 158–60
  interpersonal models and, 189–90
  medical models and, 188–89
  see also therapeutic interventions;
    therapeutic interventions, early
biological factors in mental illness:
  in diathesis-stress model, 75–76
  in era of institutionalization, 4
  explanations about, 75–77
  in psychoeducation, 35
Birley, J. L. T., 36–38
borderline personality disorder,
    65–66
Boyd, J. L., 43
Brown, G. W., 36–38
burnout, 28, 29

carelessness, 124–25
caretaking services, 146–47
"case manager" concept, 33, 207
character disorders, diagnosis of,
    65–66